170
W632bY

DISCARD
Phillips Library
Bethany College

D1557152

BETHANY
COLLEGE
LIBRARY
DISCARD

The Biology
of the Ten
Commandments

The Biology
of the Ten
Commandments
by Wolfgang Wickler
Translated by David Smith

McGRAW-HILL BOOK COMPANY
New York • St. Louis • San Francisco

English translation © 1972 by McGraw-Hill, Inc. All rights reserved. Printed in the United States of America. No part of this publication may be reproduced, stored in a retrieval system, or transmitted, in any form or by any means, electronic, mechanical, photocopying, recording, or otherwise, without the prior written permission of the publisher.

123456789BPBP798765432

Original edition: *Die Biologie der Zehn Gebote,* © R. Piper & Co. Verlag, Munich 1971.

The quotation on page 88 from PETER FREUCHEN'S BOOK OF THE ESKIMOS edited by Dagmar Freuchen is reprinted by permission of The World Publishing Company. Copyright © 1961 by Peter Freuchen Estate.

Library of Congress Cataloging in Publication Data

Wickler, Wolfgang.
    The biology of the Ten Commandments.

    Translation of Die Biologie der Zehn Gebote.
    Bibliography: p. 194
    1. Psychology, Physiological.   2. Psychology, Comparative.   3. Commandments, Ten. I. Title.
QP355.2.W513   170   72–3722
ISBN 0-07-073758-4

Contents

Introduction   1

Part 1
  Ethology and Ethics   9
  The Ethological Method   23
  The Ten Commandments   41
  Analogous Moral Behavior in Men and Animals   48
  Human Ecological Ethology
  —Who Is Our Neighbor?   63
  Digression
  What Does "Social" Mean?   70

Part 2
  Aggression Between Members of the Same Species
  —You Shall Not Kill   75
  Digression
  —Is Aggression a Spontaneous Need?   100
  Intercommunication
  —You Shall Not Lie   111
  Property
  —You Shall Not Steal   120
  Sexual Partnership
  —You Shall Not Commit Adultery   124

170
W632bY

Digression
—Who Is the Pacemaker in Evolution?   143
The Inheritance of Acquired Qualities
—Honor Your Father and Your Mother   149

Part 3
Some Biological and Ethical Conclusions   167
Love Your Neighbor as Yourself   186
Helpful Commandments   190

Bibliography   194

Introduction

MAN is a creature whose will is greater than his ability and whose ability is greater than his sense of duty. His ability, thus situated between the two poles of will and duty, is the usual object of his knowledge.

"Knowledge is power and man has achieved great power over his environment. He has not, however, gained the same power over himself and his own behavior. This has resulted in an extremely dangerous state of affairs." Konrad Lorenz wrote this in his foreword to my book on the natural laws of marriage.[71]* His view is, I believe, fundamentally correct. I do not believe, however, that this state of affairs would necessarily become any less dangerous if man were to gain more knowledge about himself and his own behavior. The danger is not to be found simply in too much or too little knowledge about everything and anything, but in man's attitude towards what he knows. I do not deny, of course, that it is better to have more knowledge than less knowledge and that a general education is better than an unbalanced one. What is decisive, however, is the use to which man puts his knowledge and his constant determination to assess and criticize himself and his own behavior. That is why my first aim in writing this book is to examine not the biological foundations of human behavior, but rather the basic principles for the correct appraisal of human behavior which can be deduced from the biological

* This and subsequent numbered notes refer to the Bibliography, p 194.

1

facts. Ethical claims which are not based on concrete biological data are meaningless.

(In parenthesis, I should point out that anyone who follows the naive allegory of creation in Genesis and thinks of man as composed of body and soul, or of mind and matter, should note that the activity of the human intellect is regarded in this book as a fundamentally biological characteristic.)

Too many people look for ready answers instead of guidelines which they might use to find answers for themselves. This is regrettable, for it reveals a dangerous and unbiological propensity for comfort. It is unbiological because it diminishes man's most characteristically human faculty of using his intellect critically. It is dangerous because it tends to make ready knowledge into a power which frequently leads to the enslavement of others, including their moral enslavement. This basically inhuman reluctance to think for oneself so often results in a confusion of knowledge and conscience and puts an alien knowledge in the place of man's individual conscience. In extreme cases, moral behavior becomes something obtainable only, as it were, on a doctor's prescription.

Knowledge is power and most people strive to achieve power. Powerful people are not, however, automatically wise or prudent, or else there would be far fewer complaints about the misuse of power.[1] Knowledge can be gained by attending educational courses, but wisdom and prudence cannot. However hard they may try to do so, the organizers of quiz games cannot give prizes for wisdom. They can only reward ready knowledge, because it is only this which will enable the competitors to give answers that are either right or wrong. It is typical that it is only by a legalistic approach that a clear decision can be made in these cases between right and wrong answer, "I don't know"

2

being ruled out. A natural scientist would allow the answer "I don't know" to pass because he, like the physician, observes phenomena and works with unexplained data. The jurist, like the moralist, presupposes a general principle and deduces his answers from it. In all trials and in the debate to establish ethical norms, the natural scientist, the physician and the psychiatrist are all consulted as experts, but the legal expert and the moralist have the last word.

Clearly, no real solution to the problem can be found in this antithesis between scientists on the one hand and lawyers and moralists on the other, but it does make the position very clear. In this book, I do not intend either to establish norms of human behavior or to act as the editor of the correspondence column in a magazine, dispensing quick answers to those who write in. Answers presuppose the existence of questions. The person who asks is seeking, and he will only escape the temptation to regard answers as more definitive than they in fact are if he continues to ask.

There is a pleasant party game with two sets of cards containing prepared questions and answers. These are drawn out in pairs, face downwards, and read aloud. The humor consists of the rigid form of the answer which never fits the question that is read out. The funny effect can be extended by inventing new questions and using the old answers. This is an amusing game. Less amusing is the reality of giving answers in life which are accepted as "universally valid." These answers are applied to every possible moral question that man may ask, but they are in fact framed as commandments, with the result that they effectively prevent further questions being asked. This is why I prefer to point to the biological situation from which such commandments may arise, because this compels us to ask many questions, including moral ones.

Anyone who has to make a decision will try to clarify

3

the material question first and regard the formal question, not as unimportant, but certainly as secondary. It is, however, easier to deal with and regularize the formal question, so that there is always a temptation to look for the support we need in form and, instead of subordinating it to the matter, raise it to the same level or even higher. In yielding to this temptation, we tend to become pharisaical in our attitude towards the traditional wording and to regard it as a tabu that may on no account be broken. In laws especially, however, what is of importance is the sense of the words, the matter, not the words themselves, the form. If we are made to feel insecure by attacks on the words used, we should remember that all that we have to lose is a false security. Our propensity for comfort favors a hardening of form, a rigid attitude towards the words themselves rather than an openness to their meaning. The only way to overcome this and to do full justice to the matter is to be critically alert at all times to these formal aspects. The man who can win through against the prevailing moral norm whenever he recognizes that this is inhuman will be acting morally. He will not be behaving morally by rebelling against the established form just for the sake of rebellion. What is essential is that "I" act. Morality is undermined by society, all the more powerfully when the individual is replaced by the anonymous "one."

Critically testing the formal framework of a law does not necessarily mean changing it. On the other hand, a change, on the basis of "always something new," does not replace the need for critical examination. This re-examination and re-interpretation of the meaning of laws presupposes, of course, a fundamental understanding. This in turn means making something so completely one's own that one can express in different words, recognize it in a different form and reinterpret it in different language.

4

The reflections that I have to offer in this book will not nourish a false pride in broken tabus or, by offering the possibility of making wrong decisions, feed a moral hangover. They may, however, indicate ways which someone who is looking for the source and meaning of human ethical norms may follow if he so wishes. The Ten Commandments provide an obvious model for this, but the method can equally well be applied to other moral laws or precepts.

PART 1

Ethology and Ethics

MAN has always compared his behavior with that of animals. Sometimes an animal is chosen as an example that is worth imitating—the busy bee, the sly fox or the cunning serpent. The man who is called a greedy pig or an old ram, on the other hand, is not regarded with admiration. Very often, of course, an animal's name is used as a term of abuse or scorn—toad, snake, rat or shrew, for instance. Domestic and farm animals and beasts that have to work for man are almost always regarded as stupid—the donkey, goose, cow or sheep and even the dog. Immanuel Kant mentioned the clever baboons in his well-known lecture on "physical geography" of 1756: "According to the Americans, these apes could talk if they wanted to, but they do not because they do not want to be compelled to work."

Many idioms and proverbs compare the observed behavior of animals with human behavior. They also contain a question about what really constitutes correct behavior—in men as well as in animals. A sixteenth-century German publication provides a good example of this. Its title is "Proverbs, fine, wise, splendid witticisms and adages. The greatest sense and wisdom of all nations and tongues, both old and new. Which must be understood and followed for the purpose of acquiring temporal and eternal prudence, virtue, education, science, knowledge, and sound management. Several thousands collected, abridged, translated into good, courtly German and explained by Sebastian Franck.

Printed at Frankfurt on the Main by Christian Egenolff.
Anno 1541." Two typical German proverbs contained in
this book and still heard often enough today are "Cats will
catch mice" (that is, "what's bred in the bone will out in
the flesh") and "(Dogs that are) great barkers are not
biters."

Opinions may, of course, differ considerably about what
constitutes "correct" behavior, but there will be general
agreement that these and other proverbs stress behavior
that is directed towards the continued existence of the
species.

It would be very remarkable if man had to depend exclusively on the animal kingdom for all his guidelines for
correct behavior. Not only the great number of possible
examples, but also their contradictory nature make it quite
impossible for him to do this. In fact, these moral comparisons are almost always poetic embellishments of demands to
which man ascribes different origins. Aristotle said, "What
art, wisdom and intellect are in man is found in animals as
a natural disposition of a similar kind." The contrast between animal instinct and human intellect is as common
today as the antithesis between impulsive and moral action.
It is frequently said that the animal *must* act correctly,
whereas man *can* do so.

In addition to this more philosophical distinction, which
relates to an exceptional human situation, there are also
other questions based on human observation and empirical
experience. One of these questions is concerned with the
causes of moral behavior. Another, equally old and indeed
venerable, but at the same time painful to many people, is
this: do ethical acts in animals and humans have similar
causes?

"Why does the hen not run away from the peacock or the
goose? She runs away from the hawk, which is smaller and

10

unknown to her. Obviously, she has foreknowledge of the harm that the hawk can cause, but she has not learnt this from experience because she is on her guard against it before she could have experienced it," Seneca wrote in one of his letters.

In 1760, Hermann Samuel Reimarus, a Protestant clergyman in Hamburg, wrote a great deal about instincts, which he called "artificial impulses." The following extracts, many of which are expressed as questions, are relevant to our theme.

The problem or main question concerning the instincts of animals is this. How is it possible for animals of every kind, lacking sense, experience, instruction, example and practice, to exercise certain regular and uniform skills almost from the moment they are born, skills which act as the most suitable means of preserving their species?

Each animal has its own element and chooses its own place to live. Each species has its own special way of making a nest, of moving about, of finding, preparing and preserving the food it likes, of protecting itself against its enemies and of mating and rearing its young.

Who teaches ducklings to go to the water as soon as they are hatched by the mother duck and to move quite differently there from the way in which they moved on the land, steering in all directions? Other animals are hatched in quite a different way, in a strange element such as the dry, hot sand and by the heat of the sun. Why do these creatures—the young turtle or crocodile—hurry from the place that has given them life straight to the water? How do they reach their food? Who teaches them to recognize their enemies? Who shows them how to use their natural weapons —horns, teeth, trunks, beaks, claws, hoofs, spines or shells—to defend themselves individually or, together with others of the same species, to their mutual advantage in attack? How do they learn to bury themselves or to seek shelter in a cave in order to hibernate undisturbed? They do not do all this simply because they love themselves or are determined to preserve themselves.

It is possible to regard mating simply as the consequence of being in heat. All the same, what is quite remarkable is firstly that no animal mates with one of another species, and secondly that the male always knows which is the female of his species. The female can neither see nor smell the one who is calling her. Who, then, tells her that this is the call of a male of her species? Who shows them the most suitable bodily position for mating, which is often quite unusual?

The question is, how is it possible for animals to act with such masterly skill for their own good and that of their species? Would it be a satisfactory answer to this question to say that nature teaches them to act in this way, that this is the consequence of their natural impulse? No, this would be making with different words an effective cause of what is regarded in the question as the effect; in other words, it would be simply playing with words.

I have quoted so many passages from Reimarus's writings because I am convinced that he is one of the great precursors of the modern science of ethology, the study of animal behavior. Many of the questions that he asked more than two hundred years ago are still unanswered today. What is perhaps more important is that he saw clearly the areas in which research had to be carried out. "It is one thing to recognize from the stimuli of the senses that something is good and therefore to desire it and another thing to know which means to use to obtain what is desirable and to put those means skillfully into effect."

But Reimarus was not only an early ethologist; he was also a theologian and a philosopher. Familiarity with the methods used in theological and philosophical argument is important because we are moving here in our attempts to define human behavior on the frontiers between biology and theology, natural science and philosophy. In this field, what matters is not so much how many facts are known as the ability to compare, contrast and use various methods of knowledge. The question is not so much *what* Reimarus

12

knew then or we know now about birds and crocodiles as *how* to combine the different ways of arguing employed in different sciences and which prejudices we have to try to remove.

From his own experience, the open-minded ethologist and observer of human and animal behavior is aware of another difference, apart from the philosophical one, between men and animals. Seneca also wrote in the same letter from which I have quoted above: "What is learned by practice develops slowly and in many different ways. What has been learned from nature itself, on the other hand, is the same in all cases and is present at the very beginning." Several related passages from Reimarus can be appended to this statement.

Although man has fewer such innate skills, he nonetheless has several that are required by the needs of his special way of life. If he is not aware of them, then he alone is to blame for being unobservant.

The Epicureans were correct to insist that children do not at first cry to excite sympathy. They arouse sympathy because adults know from their own experience that a feeling of pain is usually accompanied by such sounds.

Because they have learned the skill, adults betray their intention to communicate their passion to others by their facial expression or behavior. We cannot, however, conclude from this that children also consciously express this intention in their actions or behavior, using their innate skill. It is possible consciously and intentionally to make others aware of our passion by making such gestures and by acting in a certain way. If these actions are practiced repeatedly, they become a skill. But what is acquired by practice in this way and what is innate must be clearly distinguished. [This, one may add, also applies to animals as well as to human beings.]

The instincts of animals are not determined by nature in every aspect and so completely that nothing at all remains to be defined,

13

according to circumstances, by the animal's own capacity for knowledge . . . In this way, predatory animals seem . . . to develop a certain cunning, as to how they can best use their inborn power and their weapons to catch their prey.

Reimarus, then, regarded innate behavior—behavior which had not been acquired by learning—as that which the infant possessed from birth, but, in his opinion, the human infant was not radically different in this from the young of the higher mammals, nor was there anything in its innate behavior which made it specifically human. One distinctive feature of instinct was what he called the "determination, by means of which the mind is inclined and stirred, when the senses are stimulated in a certain way, to move certain limbs in a definite manner. I am convinced," he affirmed, "that this is the case in the arbitrary actions of children, especially their crying and sucking."

Yet two hundred years before Reimarus, Sebastian Franck listed such sayings as "What is inborn cannot be lost" and "nature is stronger than habit." As the contrast that he makes between animal and human behavior shows ("Cats will catch mice") he was not primarily referring to habits, but to natural needs which could not be suppressed. "If you cane a child on the hand for self-abuse, he will put his hand on his breast until the pain passes; but as soon as the disciplinarian has gone away, nature follows its own course again. Nature and youth cannot be restrained, even if you get the better of them for a while."[41]

The question of responsibility is at once raised by this age-old problem of human ethology. As Horace observed, "however violently nature is banished" (with a "two-pronged fork") "it always comes back." Nature is there before acquired skills. When, then, is punishment meaningful and right? What is a guilty action? What can we demand of our fellow men?

14

Reimarus went even further than this, referring to "the animal state of man, without and before the use of reason, not only in those men who have grown up among animals, but also in children before they begin to reflect and even in adults whenever they act, not according to concepts and thought, but simply in accordance with the spontaneous feelings." Finally, he observed, "if some natural and blind determination of our psychical forces or even of the inclinations of our will did not give direction to all our independent decisions, we should never be able to reach any kind of perfection."

Clearly, then, in reducing our "psychical forces" and the "inclinations of our will" to "natural and blind determination," Reimarus was trying to trace a very large part of man's activity back to biological norms that had come about in the course of human evolution. As a freethinking Christian of the Enlightenment, too, he wanted to establish a basis for religion in man's natural reason and to replace the dogmatic approach to Christian theology by the historical approach. The philosopher G. E. Lessing published extracts from Reimarus' *Apology for Rational Worshippers of God (Apologie oder Schutzschrift für die vernünftigen Verehrer Gotts)* under the title of the *Wolfenbüttel Fragments (Wolfenbütteler Fragmente)*, and these played a large part in promoting research into the historical Jesus. It is obvious, then, that the question about the origin of the norms for human behavior was first asked by, among others, a theologian more than two centuries ago within what we would now call an ethological framework.

Since then, research into animal and human behavior has continued to develop, at first imperceptibly, but later at quite an astonishing rate. Ethological studies are based on precise investigations into the lives of many different animals conducted in the first place by zoologists, who needed this knowledge in order to classify the animal kingdom

15

according to as many criteria of mutual similarity between species as could possibly be obtained. About forty or so years ago, the stage was reached when all these various observations concerning the behavior of different animals could be collected, systematized and examined with every scientific method available to see what conclusions could be drawn. The leading spirit in this work was Konrad Lorenz.

Lorenz is a physician, psychologist and zoologist. From the very beginning, he insisted that the modern science of ethology, of which he was virtually the founder, should be at the service of man and should form the basis of the study of human behavior. Although not all of the many ethologists practicing today do this, it has always been a characteristic of ethological research.

Doctors are often conscious of the fact that their patients frequently behave differently from what is normally expected—or from what would be good for themselves and their fellow-men. This raises the question whether there is any concrete cause for this and whether it can be analyzed and treated as an illness can. As it is not possible to conduct the required analytical experiments on human beings, experiments with animals form an essential part of medical research. Viruses, drugs, medicines and treatments are all regularly tried out on animals, and no patient needs to fear that he is being brought down to the level of an animal if a previously tested method helps him. Similarly, no one needs to have any fears about being regarded as less than human if ethologists make statements about biological laws concerning human behavior derived from research on animals. Such laws may well include ethical behavior, irrespective of man's freedom of choice. This freedom is not, after all, a scientifically measurable factor, and therefore cannot be revealed within a strictly scientific context.

All the same, many people are uneasy nowadays because

scientists are applying their methods to the more personal and private spheres of human life as well as to the traditional fields, such as the functions of the kidneys or the hormone glands. They are alarmed because scientists are saying that they will soon be able to know why man behaves in a particular way in a given situation and not in any other way. They are disturbed by the prospect that science may soon find an answer to the question as to how the machinery of human behavior functions in acute cases, how it has developed in the history of human society and in the lives of individuals and how it can act in special circumstances.

This uneasiness is above all caused by fear that these scientific discoveries will make it possible to interfere with the functioning of human behavior. "Manipulation" is a modern bugbear, but surely it need not inspire greater terror than the word "medicine." After all, with his detailed knowledge of the functioning of the human body, the doctor must surely be able not only to make a sick person well, but also to make a healthy person ill or a person who is already sick more sick. A knowledge of methods is neutral, even if they are methods by which human behavior might be influenced. If, however, we do not know in what direction we should influence others or what "correct" human behavior should be, then we are made to feel uncomfortable not by the increasing number of biological insights at man's disposal, but by the scantiness of his ethical insights. In these circumstances, one would expect the biologist to admit defeat in the face of this problem. I hope to show, with the help of a number of examples, why he does not capitulate and how he can in fact also deal with ethical insights. I also hope to show, in the chapters that follow, what methods can be applied and how the biologist can be acquitted of the charge of going beyond the boundaries of his own sphere of work.

17

Interestingly enough, many theologians expect biologists to cross this frontier, especially those theologians who, like Albert the Great, believe that God realizes many of his ideas in the world of creation. Their argument is that God the Creator reveals himself to the enquiring mind in nature, by directing his senseless creatures towards their goal by the natural law or by natural coercion. This accounts for the existence of "natural revelation" alongside the super-natural revelation accessible to us in Scripture and tradition. This natural revelation does not duplicate the knowledge that is revealed to us supernaturally. On the contrary, it provides us with many additional details and supplements our knowledge of God and his creative purpose. We have no other way of knowing the creative things of this world, and these can serve to show us God's will concerning how we should act and behave. In this way, our knowledge of medicine and biology as well as of ethology can have a decisive influence on the ethical insights of philosophy and theology.

The close relationship that exists between ethics and ethology, as a modern science consisting of the morphology, physiology and genetics of behavior, can be seen at once in the names themselves. The history of the two terms is also interesting in itself. Both go back, of course, to the Greek *ethos,* meaning custom or habit. From this, we derive our meaning of "morality" for ethos or ethics. The official definition of the term "ethology" given by the French Academy of Science in 1762 was "the doctrine of living customs." Thus, the task of ethology was held to be the description of facts found by man, including those that he found in himself. In 1906, ethology was called, in a leading work on human sociology, "the science of usage and customs."

In addition, the Greek *ethos* is also the basis of the word "ethology" in the sense of "science of character" in the English-speaking world, but, although this definition still appears in some dictionaries, it is completely superseded. The word "ethics," also derived from *ethos,* is, of course, related to behavior, custom and habit, but the study of ethics is not concerned with describing actions, but simply with evaluating them. In ethics, in other words, no attempt is made to compile as full a list as possible of all the moral instructions which man should obey and thereby deprive him of all freedom to decide for himself. On the contrary, it is the task of ethics to leave man as great a measure of freedom of choice as possible by giving him as much factual knowledge as he needs to enable him to make a right decision precisely in order to exercise his freedom.

Man can control nature and he can control himself, but this does not mean that he should act autocratically, arbitrarily or just as he wants to. We cannot ascertain precisely what effects one of our actions will have—this is already to a great extent present in the structure of existing creation. Not every well meaning action is successful, and ignorance and stupidity are not a very suitable norm for man's freedom or his special position.

It is interesting to conjecture what man might do if he were the Creator and had to give life to creation. Would he be able to set the laws of the structure of creation free together with its aims or optimum values, including its optimum ethical values? This, of course, is pure speculation. What is certain is that he must know the structure of existing creation if he is to manipulate its individual optimum values. To say that he can interfere in this way at all, without necessarily ruining the whole creation, is, of course, simply a working hypothesis. It is an empirical fact that it is possible to limit disturbances in creation and at least to slow down its total destruction by respecting the

19

insights that have been gained into the natural effects of creation when these are manipulated. The consequence of this is that the moral demands and the natural laws have to be identical for us as long as any insights into the effects of creation is lacking.

This is, of course, only another way of saying what the theologians mean when they express the view that, even though God's senseless creatures are incapable of gaining an insight into the effects of creation, they can reach the goal set by the Creator by means of the natural law. The more insight a living creature has, the more it is able to free itself in its ethical demands from the laws of nature. All the problems which invite man to interfere in creation for the purpose of regulating it are ultimately social problems, and for this reason we have urgent need of insights into the natural laws of social life. These natural laws, however, are found in different degrees of validity. There are, for example, general laws and particular laws. Because our scientific knowledge almost always proceeds from the particular to the general, today's truth tends, as Otto Koehler said, to become tomorrow's special case.

In our quest for general laws, we should never be satisfied with what we already know. In our search for social laws, we must begin with special cases and then continue our search with great determination. Every aspect of our study is necessarily tentative—including the conclusions that are drawn in this book—and the individual examples offered here are in themselves far less important than the general tendency that they disclose and the place that these occupy in our total vision.

We are bound to be modest in our claims in this sphere because our ethological investigations into social organisms are only at a beginning; and so far we have only considered those creatures which are biologically very close to man—

in other words, vertebrates. There are more than a million different known species of animal life, however, and only six per cent of these are vertebrates. Since it is hardly possible to maintain that the remaining ninety-four per cent tell us nothing about nature or the plan of creation, research will certainly have to be done into the behavior of those creatures which are more remote from man, even though we may be exclusively interested in the natural laws to which man is subject. We may therefore conclude that at least one fundamental demand must be satisfied whenever norms are laid down for moral behavior.

It is this: in any attempt to proclaim moral norms, we must be careful to recognize the natural laws to which man is subject and from which he cannot escape, but which he must turn to his advantage whenever he tries to fulfill these norms. The natural laws underlying human behavior and which can be known by using the methods of the natural scientist enable us to control creation and human nature, insofar as this follows the laws of nature. They are also well adapted to the task of making it easier for man to act in accordance with these moral norms. More than this, however, they actually provide guidelines—restrictive guidelines, at least—for the postulation of norms according to which man ought to act.

In the pages that follow, I will attempt to show why criticism of social norms (though not necessarily their discovery) is a job that specifically belongs to the ethologist. His long-term goal, let us say, is to test ethical norms against natural laws—perhaps even to trace them back to natural laws. This does not mean, however, that nothing should be demanded of man that may go beyond the known laws of nature. In my opinion, the Christian commandment of love (see p. 186ff.) goes far beyond the natural laws. If, however, we are to justify any such "higher aim," we must make use

21

of arguments at the level of the laws of nature which show clearly why it is possible and permissible for man to leave this purely natural sphere.

If these arguments are not forthcoming, the ethical directive may still be correct, but—strictly speaking—it should not be followed. I will try to explain why this is so when I come to discuss the problem of authority. At the same time, I shall also have to explain the nature of the natural laws in behavior, to which reference has been made so often in this chapter, and my justification for including man in this consideration. It seems to me to be important, however, to establish from the outset the fact that an attempt to evaluate behavior ethically does not replace an exact knowledge and analysis of behavior. On the contrary, such knowledge is a prerequisite for any evaluation.

The Ethological Method

THE question that was asked by Aristotle, Seneca, Reimarus and others concerning the "right" behavior of animals provides the point of departure for a great deal of ethological research today. If the behavior in question is in accordance with the situation, this may be seen as pure chance, or it may be a mystery. The first pronouncement can be eliminated because of the frequency of the phenomenon; the second can only be accepted by the scientist as an excuse, never as an explanation. After all, he could always fall back on the idea of the mystery and simply stop doing research. In fact, however, without denying its existence, he puts it to one side and uses as a working hypothesis the theory that adjustments between the organism and its environment—and more especially the behavior of the organism—are based on adaptive processes on the part of the organisms themselves. The adaptability of behavior is quite certainly one of the fundamental questions facing ethologists in Europe today; Konrad Lorenz has recently published a detailed study devoted to this question.[37]

It is clearly not possible to assume that everything that fits does so by virtue of a process of adaptation directed towards this special adjustment. Research workers in the field of ethology tend to overlook the fact that one process of adaptation often brings other adjustments in its wake as side-effects. As a result, they often come across new "problems."

There is, for example, the theory according to which in-

23

sects, crabs and spiders change their way of walking if they lose one or more legs, with the result that they continue to move in a suitably coordinated manner with the remaining legs. If this early theory is true, it means that these animals have special patterns of movement in reserve which they can use in all possible situations, according to how many and which legs are lost. The question is, then, where do these different coordinates come from? It would be contrary to all we know of biology to assume that every combination of incomplete sets of legs occurred often enough for it to be worthwhile for each lower creature to develop every possible reserve coordinate of movement in addition to its normal coordinate.

If, however, the mechanism of such a creature's normal movement is very carefully analyzed, it is seen that this mechanism consists of individual, balanced and coordinated circular movements which influence each other according to definite laws and which automatically produce observed coordinates in what is left of the legs that have been lost.[67] What looks like a very sophisticated special adaptation, then, is in reality a secondary effect of the original adaptation. We must consider that adaptations of this kind may also occur as side effects at the higher level of behavioral physiology. (I have dealt with this problem in greater detail elsewhere, in a discussion of the emergence of communication between animals, the influence of behavior on bodily structure and the phenomenon of ritualization.)[73]

The question of the adaptability of behavior is raised again and again and every time it is reduced to one of three possible regions of adjustment. In other words, if we take as our point of departure the simple observation that each organism acts differently according to the situation in which it is placed, but that its behavior is always adequate to meet the needs of that situation, we will note that the organism needs to meet three requirements for survival.

24

Firstly, an animal must be able to recognize the given situation (friend, enemy or object to be dealt with) by certain features. In other words, it has to know how to distinguish essential characteristics from less important ones. Secondly, it has to be able to coordinate the various muscles, organs, movements and contributory actions that are necessary if it is to behave correctly in this situation. Thirdly, it must select, from its repertory of possible modes of behavior, one which is suitable to the given situation and suppress the others.

We may give a simple example, that of the frog catching a fly. The frog has to "know" three things. In the first place, it has to know what a fly looks like. (It has to be able to distinguish the fly from other objects.) In the second place, it must know how to coordinate the movement of its legs, mouth and tongue to make the catch. In the third place, it must be aware that it has to catch the fly and not simply croak at it or threaten it.

If these elements are not clearly distinguished and we simply ask whether the frog's catching of a fly or the chaffinch's nest-building in the spring is innate or acquired, then there would be every justification to reject the question as unanswerable. It may well be, after all, that the individual animal acquires the information that it needs in order to adapt its behavior in two out of three of these possible zones of adaptation, either traditionally or by experience. At the same time, it may be that it is only in the third of these regions that its adaptation is hereditary—or "instinctive," as it would have been called in the past.

The ethologist, then, tries to understand how a "living system"—either a unicellular organism or a whole society or colony of cells—functions. This is why he is brought more and more, in his field of research, into contact with all the other disciplines that are concerned with the task of throwing light on the structure, function and history of

25

parts of living systems (sense organs, muscles, hormones, nerves, genes and so on). Since these structural parts never occur, under natural conditions, individually, but only in connection with each other as living organisms, the ethologist examines those units which are in fact subject to selection and evolution, with the result that his field of research most closely conforms to what is commonly understood nowadays as zoology. This means that he has to take into account not only the animal that he is studying as an independent organism, but also its normal environment and its special historical background. Let me quote Pastor Reimarus once again in this context.

It seems to me that many doubts must exist concerning the history of individual animals, especially tame or captive animals. It is, after all, impossible to know the exact circumstances of particular events and data in their lives and, because of this, it is probable that these data would be wrongly interpreted. If animals are not living in a state of natural freedom, no conclusions about their natural impulses can be drawn from their actions because these impulses are partly extinguished and partly changed in the animals' artificial way of life . . . But whereas the actions of tame or trained animals are not the outcome of purely natural impulses, the behavior of wild animals living in freedom is something that is very difficult indeed to observe. A great deal of artifice and care has to be exercised if animals are to be watched and heard in their natural and concealed state. I have therefore made it a rule never to trust anyone, even the most modern naturalist, unless he tells me explicitly the way he arrived at his observations.

It needs hardly be said that this warning applies equally well today. But how does the ethologist observe animals, and how does he draw conclusions from what he has observed?

COLLECTING

Ideally, he will observe as many different species as possible over as long a period as possible. The animals will, of course, usually be in captivity, so that he can follow the more detailed aspects of their behavior as closely as possible. This is easy enough in the case of small animals, but more difficult with larger species, because, if they are to be normally active, they need more room than can be provided in ordinary cages or enclosures. Certain large animals can, however, be left free in a semi-wild state, or be observed in natural surroundings. This is necessary in any case in order to amplify the information acquired in captivity. However, such sanctuaries are not always ideal, and animals living in this way are often very shy of man. What is more, if the social patterns of animal behavior are to be observed, as many animals as possible must be individually known and they must be watched for long periods.

Attempts have frequently been made to achieve this ideal. In 1836, for example, Frédéric Cuvier called for the institution of a chair in animal psychology, but was not successful because Isidore Saint-Hilaire pleaded with greater success for a chair in general zoology. A hundred years later, the question was made acute again in France, when there was a clear desire in the nineteen-thirties to use the animals in the Vincennes Zoo for scientific purposes.[65] In 1933, a professorship in ethology was set up in Paris, but the emphasis was still on wild animals in captivity. It is only very recently that a beginning has been made with wild animals in the field. The complicated nature of field work and the enormous amount of time involved in this type of research—a wild goose can live for sixty years—are the main reasons why we still know so very little about most wild animals. The results that have thus far been

27

achieved are very promising, but they are incomplete and great care has to be exercised in drawing conclusions.

MEASURING

Another important aspect of the study of animal behavior is the exact measurement of what is usually known as an impulse. The ethologist has to insist that an impulse be directly or indirectly measurable if it is to be capable of physiological investigation. In the physiology of behavior, an impulse is above all what underlies a series of actions. The word "motivation" is also used and the analysis and measurement of the structure of an impulse is also known as motivation analysis. This hypothetical structure called an impulse or motivation is measurable as a readiness on the part of an organism to carry out a specific action. It is, for example, possible to tie a belt attached to a spring around a hungry animal and so measure the strength of the animal's impulse to obtain food that is out of its reach. Another way of measuring the impulse to reach food is to stretch wires charged with electricity of different strengths across the path between the animal and the food and record the maximum strength of current that the animal will overcome in order to feed. Both of these experiments provide measurements of the impulse to reach food or of food motivation. The longer the time since the animal's last meal, the harder it will pull on the spring or the greater the discomfort it will endure from the electrical currents. It is equally possible to measure the quantity of food that is consumed in a meal, by weighing the animal before and after eating and to test quite accurately the degree to which the food has to be made unpalatable before the hungry animal refuses to touch it. These measurements will also provide us

28

with quite an accurate analysis of the animal's state of hunger and his urge to appease it.

A sexually aroused animal, on the other hand, will not be attracted by food, but can be made to respond quite easily to an animal of the opposite sex because he is motivated to mate, not to seek food. This impulse is also measurable.

An intimidated animal which is ready to run away will, of course, be unlikely to react to food, even if it is hungry. It will, however, respond quickly to flight stimuli. This shows that one impulse can influence another and in certain cases even suppress it altogether. In addition, each impulse is characterized by a certain mode of behavior. The impulse to feed is marked by eating behavior, the nesting impulse by the collection of materials to build a nest and the urge to mate by special display, calls or other mating behavior. It is quite possible to deduce from the frequency of these different modes of behavior the nature and the strength of the impulse in each case.

I do not propose to discuss in greater detail the many different methods used for measuring these impulses—full information will be found, for example, in Eibl-Eibesfeldt's recent manual on comparative ethology.[10] Generally speaking, we may say that impulses can be measured and distinguished from each other and that it is possible to state how many variable impulses which are independent of each other there are in a given species of animal, and which of the visible modes of behavior depend on which impulse.

This has been known for a long time, of course. Yet there are still scholars of a belligerent turn of mind who are reluctant to accept the fact that research into animal behavior can be of value to man both from the ethological and from the medical point of view. Hannah Arendt, for example, recently had this to say of ethological research:

29

"Clearly, what we have here is no longer a science, but a theory based on hypotheses which is highly suspect because it is concerned to such an extent with physical concepts—energy and the storage of energy—which are highly questionable when applied to biological and physiological data because they cannot be measured."[1]

She refuses to have anything to do with the "rather off-handed conclusions" of zoologists "which have nonetheless convinced a large number of people and have given rise to new sciences." She herself believes that the "net result of all this research is that violence and aggressiveness seem more 'natural' and that the latter is given a much more important part to play in human society than we should be ready to accept without the former." She is convinced that "these results are very undesirable and not at all in accordance with the observed phenomena themselves." To quote her own words, they are "seen from a so-called 'humanist' point of view, without any background of 'research.'" She claims that ethologists have been trying either to justify or to condemn the behavior of men on the basis of that of animals: "The criterion for human behavior is derived from the behavior of other genera."

I hope to be able to show in the chapters that follow that this is certainly not the case. But Hannah Arendt not only confuses the objective analysis and measurement of impulses that are being made at present with ethical evaluation; she also quite wrongly accuses ethologists of claiming "that the additional gift of reason only upsets the physiological mechanisms of the human structure of instincts." This is why, she insists, "scientists feel impelled nowadays to cure us of these side-effects of the intellect, not so much by trying to control our instincts, as by re-orienting them. The objects of man's instincts have to be replaced by substitutes and the instincts themselves directed towards com-

30

pensatory achievements after the intervention of the intellect has led to the loss of their original function in the normal economy of nature."

She does not attempt to conceal her regret that "zoologists, biologists and physiologists are now virtually dominating a field which only a few decades ago was occupied mainly by psychologists, sociologists and political scientists." She does, however, avoid making any comparison between the methods and working hypotheses used in the two areas of study which she contrasts with each other. I am personally convinced that working hypotheses, whatever their origin, need only be shunned by those who favor hypotheses of pure convenience. And I hardly need to point out that Hannah Arendt is quite mistaken in her assertion that energy directed towards a specific action and the strength of an impulse are not measurable.

COMPARING

In this context, the particularly important field of work is known as "comparative ethology." In this work, three elements are compared: characteristics, species and performances.

By comparing characteristics, we acquire information about the way in which individual organs or modes of behavior have developed—how, for example, the front leg of a saurian has become a bird's wing or the flipper of a whale, or how a young animal's begging movement develops into a greeting between adults. If we compare species together with the characteristics of different species, we can discover how these species have evolved from each other and this type of research has, of course, led to the compilation of genealogical trees of living organisms. Both the comparison

31

of characteristics and the comparison of species include natural similarities and have as their aim the discovery of affinities of origin and descent.

The comparison of performances provides us with information about different organs and modes of behavior that are able to carry out the same tasks. We can learn, for example, how eyes have evolved quite independently in groups of animals which are not closely related to each other—in vertebrates, cephalopods and insects—or which modes of behavior are employed as calming gestures by birds, carnivores, ungulates or apes. This comparison of performances includes functionally conditioned similarities and has as its aim the discovery of affinities of adaptation.

Affinities of origin and descent are known as *homologies,* whereas similarities based on adaptation are called *convergences.* Research into homologies is different in its methods from the study of convergences, which shows us what has developed similarly, although it has often evolved from very different origins, in the case of a certain performance. A good example of research in this field is the attempt to discover which qualities are essential to a wing that is suitable for flying. In the study of homologies, on the other hand, the ethologist investigates the origin of the structural material used in certain concrete cases to achieve the structural principle; in other words, he tries to ascertain from which parts of the body and in which ways the wings of an insect, a bird or a bat have developed.

The study of homologies and research into convergences are mutually complementary. Up until recently, however, the study of homologies has occupied such a prominent place in ethology that far too little is known about convergences. This is lamentably clear from the conclusions which have been reached by many ethologists from their observation of animals and which have been applied by them to human behavior.

Above all, it is the behavior of the animals that are most closely related to man, in other words, the anthropoid apes, that is observed and the results of these studies that are regarded as decisive in any attempt to acquire information about the biology of human behavior. Very rarely are the results gained from observing the behavior of creatures more remote from man taken so seriously. Again and again, especially in reviews of our more popular scientific books, we come across the criticism—directed even by prominent journalists—that we should study the anthropoid ape rather than draw hair-raising conclusions from our research on animals such as the chaffinch or the perch. Man, these writers claim, is a primate and not a kind of goose, and the ethologist should therefore either concern himself with fields directly related to human problems or else admit that his science is no more than an esoteric hobby which has no contribution to make to the question of man's continued existence.

What these critics fail to recognize is that the evolution of species reveals ecological niches in just the same way as a study of economics discloses deficiencies in the market. Related species avoid each other as competitors like similar products of the same firm. The market researcher who wants to familiarize himself with the typical and functional characteristics of a product will therefore investigate not the other products of the same firm, but rather the products of some completely different firm which are aimed at the same market, the same group of consumers.

Anyone who is interested in the biological laws of monogamy in man would therefore be advised not to study the habits of the chimpanzee, whose environment is quite different from that of man—so different, in fact, that man has the greatest difficulty in following him there as an observer —and whose social system has evolved along quite different lines from that of man. On the contrary, he would be wiser to study the lives of monogamous organisms taken from a completely dissimilar group of animals. If he did this, he would find out the conditions under which monogamy flourishes and the other biological qualities that usually appear when monogamy is present. The study of convergences conducted with as many different species as possible provides a good knowledge of the functional characteristics of animals, whereas what is learned from a study of homologies in closely related species is how the structure required was evolved in concrete cases. This is why the knowledge gained from a study of convergences is more fundamental than that acquired from research into homologies. This also applies to problems which have customarily been regarded as exclusively human, as I hope to demonstrate in the chapters that follow.

There is, however, another important reason why convergences have to be studied if research into animal behavior is to be of any use to man. The results of research into one species of organism can never be transferred to another organism. Only a working hypothesis can be transferred. One species cannot be investigated as completely representative of another. All that one can hope for is that certain similarities of a general nature will be found in certain parts in the case of parallel investigations, and that this method can be to some extent perfected so that it may point towards the answer that one is looking for.

Medical research workers do not try out their techniques or drugs on rats because men are rodents, but because it has been proved that rats (and several other animals) react, in many physiological spheres, similarly to men. As a result of experiments with rats, however, it is only possible to formulate working hypotheses and make probability statements about the possible effect of the drug on man. The most notorious and tragic case of a wrong forecast, but not the only one, was the Thalidomide affair.

34

After experimenting, for example, with rats, doctors next try out their working hypotheses very cautiously on human beings by testing the new drugs, once they have been subjected to all the preliminary tests, directly on man. This direct experiment is, of course, conducted with every possible precaution, but it cannot be avoided. On the basis of his experiments, the doctor knows which species of test animal will yield the safest forecasts of the effect of his treatment on human beings. The ethologist does not even know this much. All that he knows is that not every species is equally suitable for model testing. But it has not been possible to date to verify which species provide the working hypotheses that can most usefully be applied to man, because such vast sections of the whole individual life of the species in question and of the social life of the species would have to be examined and checked.

Of course, attempts are made to investigate quasi-experimental results by means of comparisons and by making use of whatever social abuses and individual misfortunes are available, but it is never possible to include all the factors that may play a part. Experimentation can be replaced by collecting cases, but the fewer the cases, the less adequate they are as a substitute. Like confessors, psychiatrists and doctors are always in danger of learning above all about abnormal, pathological cases and therefore of acquiring no deeper knowledge of the biologically normal state. The ethologist has so far not run this risk, because he is almost exclusively interested in the biologically normal, healthy animal—to such an extent, in fact, that his neglect of abnormalities may even be regarded as dangerous. This is why he is almost always unable to help those who come to him for advice about breeding domestic animals and overcoming the disturbing peculiarities of behavior that occur so often as the result of the modern methods of intensive rearing of animals.

35

Because he cannot say with absolute certainty which animals will be ideally suited for tests, the ethologist has to safeguard himself and to find statements which have sufficient universal and representative validity to form the basis for a safe forecast of human behavior. He will not, of course, learn in this way what is specifically human, but he will come to understand some of the essential aspects of the structure of human functions which man has in common with other living organisms. The broader the basis on which such experiments are carried out, the more reliable the conclusions will be and the more cases of convergence these tests contain, the more certain we can be about functional characteristics. Thus I cannot accept as valid the procedure followed by F. Frank,[15] who has based his conclusions on an arbitrary collection of examples.

The sociologist is in very much the same position as the ethologist. Once he has completed the process of collecting and ordering his material, he has to conduct tests in order to understand the sociological laws that he has discovered. If he does not use experimental methods, he will be working under an illusion. If, on the other hand, he wants to avoid experimenting on human beings at least for as long as he can, he will inevitably have to depend on models and comparisons with animals. This is a principle that was recognized almost a hundred years ago by a little-known Lettish sociologist, Paul von Lilienfeld,[33] in his analysis of language and concepts published originally in 1873 (a publication which was, in many respects, marked by one-sidedness). "Human society is," he claimed emphatically, "like natural organisms, a real being." He also insisted that "much that has hitherto been regarded as belonging to the ideal world undeniably forms part of the real world." "Everything in human society is based, like everything in nature, on mutual interaction and not on absolute principles." "The student

36

of human society is in the position of a passive, outside observer. He is like a spiritual anatomist." The sociologist has therefore to employ the "inductive and empirical method, progressing from the particular to the general"—the usual method in the natural sciences—and he will find thereby that "much that has taken place in human society which was ascribed in the past to the direct activity of God could now legitimately be explained on the basis of natural causes and the universally recognized laws of the evolution of society. Many of these events would therefore be seen as only indirectly attributable to God."

Even at the present stage in the development of ethological studies, it is important to continue to collect as much evidence as possible, so as to gain a wide view of the possibilities that exist in nature. If some of these elements of behavior discovered in animals are also found to play a part in man, the ethologist has to try to learn more about them in the animals he is investigating. What he has to find out especially is the connection between these modes of behavior and various external and internal factors. He also has to discover which of these factors ultimately determine the behavior. Research in this area can only succeed if two conditions are fulfilled. The first is that the element of behavior or the situation in question has to be identifiable and recognizable beyond all doubt. The second condition is that the methods used by the researcher must be stated clearly and precisely enough for his results to be tested and reproduced. This is, of course, one of the fundamental principles of all research into the natural sciences; as Reimarus wrote, we would not "trust even the most modern naturalist, unless he indicates the way he arrived at his observations."

This methodological problem is particularly acute in the question of killing a member of the same species and of aggression in general (see p. 75ff.). How many individuals of the same species have to be investigated before a generalized statement can justifiably be made about all the others that have not been examined, in other words, about the species as a whole? How many species have to be investigated before the conclusion can be drawn that the universal phenomenon of "aggression" exists at all? It is dangerous and unscientific to take the second step before the first and to interpret a phenomenon in the very name that we give to it. In other words, we must above all be on our guard against simply speaking about "attack" before describing the mode of behavior so carefully that it can be clearly and unmistakably recognized by other scientists, who will then be able to decide for themselves what criteria are to be applied to determine "attack behavior."

The scientist should not only have the fullest possible list of empirical data at his disposal. He must also be able to understand as fully as possible the laws governing the behavior of the organism he is studying. In this case, he will be able to predict with some degree of certainty the behavior of the organism under different conditions. His forecasts about situations that have not yet been investigated can in this way act as the touchstone for scientific working hypotheses.

If the aim is to investigate the behavior of animals—and especially that of higher animals—scientifically along these lines, then all the factors which may influence that behavior in any way must be very carefully checked. This can be done in two ways. Either all these factors have to be measured, or they have all to be eliminated with the exception of the one that is to be examined. We have to be practical here, of course, and so it is better to speak not of "all" these factors, but rather of the most important of them. After all, we simply do not know all the factors and it is difficult

38

enough to check only the most important of those that we do know. But the significance of any scientific statement is limited by the part played by these factors that can be and are in fact checked.

By "checking," of course, we usually mean any form of measuring. We may say, then, that the natural scientist is only really interested in what he can measure in some way. This does not only imply a strict application of the metric system. It also means that we have to be open to the positive value of scales of comparison of the kind used by the historian or the specialist in phylogeny. Both methods can be employed, if necessary, to check and measure the correctness of statements about processes that have taken place in the past.

The main problem, then, is to be found not in the sphere of subjective understanding, intuition, empathy or experience, but in that of mutual communication and agreement between individual men about something. Science is first and foremost the result of mutual agreement about what is subjectively known, and this agreement can only be reached if what is known is reduced to variables which have been established on the basis of mutual agreement. These variables are sometimes known by the Greek word "parameters." No problem is involved in man's purely subjective experience of some phenomenon as valuable, beautiful or right. Where a serious problem is at once raised, however, is when we attempt to find out whether these subjective feelings are the same in different individuals or whether they can be produced in different individuals by the same data.

This, then, is why progress came to be made in the natural sciences as soon as the method of reaching agreement about natural data became clear to scientists. Little progress was made as long as nature was simply contemplated subjectively or mystically. Anything that cannot be investigated by scientific methods must inevitably be regarded as something that does not concern the scientist. Anyone who believes that subjective human values are bound to disappear from sight whenever an attempt is made to examine them as individual factors that can be measured scientifically, should not expect the scientist to investigate these values. Indeed, he should not ask the scientist to make any statement at all about whether these values exist or not.

The Ten Commandments

BOTH in the Old and the New Testaments, the Ten Commandments were generally accepted as the basis and the quintessence of morality, and there is still widespread acceptance of them as a norm today. These commandments are usually formulated in the following way:

1. You shall have no other gods before me.
2. You shall not take the name of the Lord your God in vain.
3. Remember the sabbath day, to keep it holy.
4. Honor your father and your mother.
5. You shall not kill.
6. You shall not commit adultery.
7. You shall not steal.
8. You shall not bear false witness against your neighbor.
9. You shall not covet your neighbor's wife.
10. You shall not covet your neighbor's goods.

Historical research has provided us with a great deal of important information about these commandments, so that it is no longer difficult to understand them. (I am particularly indebted to Herbert Haag[19] in this respect.) The formulation of the commandments has, like all traditional material, passed through a long process of development, which can be followed to a great extent within the Bible itself.

In the book of Exodus, which begins with an account of the Israelites' leaving Egypt, the list opens with four commandments directly related to God (Exodus 20. 2–8):

1. You shall have no other gods before me.

41

2. You shall not make for yourself any image of God.

3. You shall not take the name of the Lord your God in vain.

4. Remember the sabbath day, to keep it holy.

These are followed by the commandments listed above, beginning with the fourth and ending with the tenth, which in Exodus reads: "You shall not covet your neighbor's house; you shall not covet your neighbor's wife, or his manservant, or his maidservant, or his ox, or his ass, or anything that is your neighbor's." In the seventh and sixth centuries, at the time of the later book, Deuteronomy, also known as the fifth Book of Moses, the wife was no longer regarded as part of the man's house and goods. She is therefore listed, in Deuteronomy, before the man's house and goods, in the Ninth Commandment. In accordance with the attitude towards society which characterizes the whole of this later book, the wife is raised from the level of a thing to that of a person. The number ten of the Decalogue is preserved by the amalgamation of the first and second commandments of the earlier version.

To the Semitic mind, the number ten was the quintessence of totality. Even now, Judaism prescribes that there must be a minimum of ten men present, legally representing the totality of the community, before an official service can be held. There were ten plagues of Egypt and God revealed the totality of his power in them. Similarly, he manifested the totality of his divine will in the Ten Commandments, which are the central articles of the Torah, the Mosaic law, and had to be interpreted in accordance with changing times and circumstances.

At the time of Christ, the Jew had to observe six hundred and thirteen individual commandments of the law, yet Jesus' answer to the rich young man who asked him what he had to do to win eternal life was a radical summary of this complicated code. "You know the commandments," he said, " 'Do not kill, Do not commit adultery, Do not steal, Do not bear false witness, Do not defraud, Honor your father and mother' " (Mark 10. 17–19). What is remarkable in this summary is that it does not contain the first three (or four) commandments that are directly concerned with God. Since they are not directly related to man and human society, I will also leave these first commandments out and confine myself to the "social" commandments which regularly appear together in pictorial or sculptured representations on the stone tablets of the law.

Long before Moses, in the Egypt of the New Kingdom from the sixteenth to the twelfth centuries, a book of the dead was buried with the deceased man, containing formulae which amount to protestations of innocence to Osiris, the judge of the dead and the god of the hereafter. Many of these formulae are very similar to those contained in the Decalogue:

"I have not done wrong.
I have not robbed.
I have not been avaricious.
I have not stolen.
I have not killed men.
I have not reduced the corn measure.
I have not uttered lies."

It is clear from this that the Israelites were not alone in making moral demands. Furthermore, these were not maximal demands, but basic demands which could be fulfilled relatively easily by everyone. Theologians are generally agreed that the Decalogue restricts itself to serious sins.

What is more, the Decalogue also served as the text of the making of a covenant—customary in the Ancient Near East, but in this case between God and his people. The form of address "you" therefore applies above all to the part-

43

ner in this covenant, the whole people of Israel. The Decalogue, then, was not dealing in the first place with offenses that the individual might commit, but rather with transgressions which Israel as a whole should not commit and should not tolerate among her people—offenses which would be punishable in other codes of law by death. The essence of this text of the covenant had to be proclaimed again and again, usually in the liturgy, and it had to be expressed apodeictically in short sentences with a similar pattern and sound that could be easily grasped and even learned by heart by those who heard them.

It is also obviously necessary to enlarge on such terse, easily memorized formulae and to explain them so that they could be applied to everyday life at different periods. The situation in which the people, clan or tribe was placed at any given time is reflected in these explanations and amplifications of the law. In the book of Exodus, for example, we find that the chapter which precedes the one containing the Ten Commandments includes a description of the arrival of the wandering tribes in the Sinai desert. In the commandment concerning the Sabbath, however, we read: "You shall not do any work . . . or the sojourner within your gates." This clearly does not apply to Israel when the people were nomads, but to the people as a settled community. What we have here is an amplification appended later to the original formula of the commandment. The most important differences between the two biblical versions of the Decalogue are often to be found in these extensions.

It is interesting to compare the ten biblical commandments with the commandments of the Masai, who still live as cattle-breeding nomads in the steppes of East Africa. As early as 1910, Moritz Merker[42] wrote a detailed study of the traditions of the Masai, in which he pointed to astonishing parallels with the early history of the Hebrews, including a similar tradition of law-giving on a mountain. Apparently, these Masai are descended from the same people as the earliest Hebrews, and they have preserved the more original version of the commandments because they have remained nomadic. The Masai commandments are:

1. You shall not make for yourself any image of God.
2. You shall not kill any people.
3. You shall not take the possessions of any other Masai.
4. You shall agree with each other and not quarrel with each other.
5. No man shall touch the wife of a married man.
6. If a Masai has lost his property, the others shall support him.
7. Only one shall rule over you.
8. A man shall always have only one wife.
9. You shall not kill any female animals.

The tenth commandment prescribes two religious feasts in the year. (The Israelites had more than seventy feast days in the year on which they had to rest—something that no cattle-breeding people can afford to do.)

All these Masai commandments are familiar to us in the same or at least in similar form from the numerous and often very detailed instructions given in first books of the Old Testament. This is why Merker concluded: "The biblical author inserted new laws that had become necessary or modifications of existing laws that had arisen because the people had changed their outlook and their way of life as a result of becoming settled into the traditional framework of the ancient legislation. At the same time and for the same reason, he also left out commandments that had become lost or had been displaced from their privileged position because of their diminished importance."

One has only to look at the other series of ten commandments that is also included in the book of Exodus to know

45

that Merker was right. This series of commandments is distinguished from the so-called "ethical" Decalogue by, among other things, the inclusion of many elements concerned with cattle breeding. It is known as the "cultic" Decalogue (Exodus 34. 10–26).

1. You shall worship no other God.
2. You shall make for yourself no molten gods.
3. The feast of unleavened bread you shall keep.
4. All that opens the womb is mine, all your male cattle, the firstlings of cow and sheep.
5. On the seventh day you shall rest; in plowing time and in harvest you shall rest.
6. Three times in the year shall all your males appear before the Lord God, the God of Israel.
7. You shall not offer the blood of my sacrifice with leaven;
8. Neither shall the sacrifice of the feast of the passover be left until the morning.
9. The first of the first fruits of your ground you shall bring to the house of the Lord your God.
10. You shall not boil a kid in its mother's milk.

(In passing, it may be noted that there is only one way of declining to accept an invitation to share in a—for us not always very appetizing—Masai meal without offending the host. This is to say that you have already taken either meat or milk. The Masai still refuse, even nowadays, to consume both on the same day and thus mix them.)

We may therefore conclude that, as far as we can tell from our knowledge of history and tradition, man has always had ethical commandments. What is more, both the precise formulation of these and the choice of the ten most important have changed according to time and circumstance. Seen in this perspective, an adaptation of the commandments to different situations is undoubtedly justified.

We shall have to consider later the conditions under which this adaptability is not merely arbitrary or does not lead to misguided situational ethics. It is in the meantime not too difficult to justify the comparison that I have made here between the Decalogue and already existing natural, biological laws. At the time of Moses, after all, there was no conscious distinction made between divine and natural laws. All laws were regarded as an expression of God's will.

Analogous Moral Behavior
in Men and Animals

THE biological laws according to which animals behave and human beings should behave can be regarded as different ways of expressing the same creative will. They may, on the other hand, not be seen in this light. What is certain, however, is that it is impossible to ignore the many aspects they have in common—aspects which were not in the first place discovered by modern ethologists.

In the eighteenth century, there was an increasing tendency to apply the methods hitherto used exclusively in the natural sciences to research into the social life of man. It very soon became clear then that man's social life followed certain natural laws. The founder of modern sociology, Auguste Comte, resolved in 1822 to look for the "unchanging natural laws" to which human society was subject. He therefore tried to move forward from mathematics to astronomy, physics, chemistry and biology and beyond these natural sciences to psychology, which he regarded as an aspect of physiology, and then even further to an ultimate science to which he, significantly, gave the name of "social physics."

"I shall deal with the conditions of man's social existence," he stated, "in the way in which I dealt with the organized structure of the body under the title of 'anatomy' in biology. I shall then deal with the laws of social movement in the way in which I discussed the laws of life in biology under the title of 'physiology.' This division into statics and dynamics is necessary in order to employ it for as long as it is useful."

The name "social physics" had, however, already been used before by the Belgian statistician Adolphe Quételet in 1835, who applied statistical methods to social phenomena and especially to moral qualities. On the basis of statistical evidence about crimes on the one hand and extremely courageous activities on the other, Quételet concluded that men and women in Germany, France and Flanders, whom he grouped according to age and professional status, had certain propensities towards certain types of activity. Clearly, he was attempting to assess moral qualities and was doing so by measuring the effects of these qualities, just as ethologists today measure readiness to perform certain actions. Quételet went even further, looking for indicators in which propensities which had not yet been changed into actions could be observed. This still remains a very acute problem in sociological research.

The theory underlying his research was, however, not at all attractive to many of his contemporaries. This theory can best be described by the image of bullet holes on a target. Most of the shots are concentrated around the bull's-eye and there are fewer and fewer further away from the center. Quételet believed, for example, that most human beings were, as far as their size was concerned, concentrated like bullet holes around the center, the natural size of the body which was nature's target. The giants and the dwarfs, on the other hand, were like shots that were wide of the mark—they became fewer and fewer the further away they were in size from the bull's-eye, the size aimed at by nature.

In other words, the average, the middle size that occurred most frequently, was regarded by Quételet as the target aimed at by nature or, in the case of many of man's *moral* qualities, as the target aimed at by society.

This, of course, at once raises the question as to whether the average is not being confused with what is desirable and what is normal with the norm.[57] The title of a book published in 1867 and written by the German mathematician and philosopher Moritz Wilhelm Drobisch is very characteristic of this type of conclusion drawn from statistical research—*Moral Statistics and Human Free Will* (*Die moralische Statistik und die menschliche Willensfreiheit*). Quételet, however, was above all concerned with the question of describing and measuring phenomena, and not with that of finding criteria for their moral evaluation. Describing the average citizen or the average Christian and measuring the qualities that have been discovered in him does not necessarily mean that we want him to be average.

In 1741, a Protestant pastor in Prussia, Johann Peter Süssmilch,[61] published a book on the "divine order in the changes that have taken place in the human race, from the birth, death and reproduction of the race" (*Die göttliche Ordnung in den Veränderungen des menschlichen Geschlechts, aus der Geburt, Tod, und Fortpflanzung desselben*). It is clear from the title of this book that the author regarded the "divine order" as responsible for statistical laws. Even now, more than two hundred years later, many people are still convinced that God, whose ways are inscrutable, wanted this or that to happen just as it did happen. The more frequently something does happen in just that way, the more normal it seems to us. The process which enables us, for example, to adapt ourselves to an average expectation of life or to an average summer temperature in the country in which we live is interpreted by such people as resignation to the will of God. If this attitude fails to spur men on to greater activity, then it is—even from the theological point of view (in a world that has not yet been "consummated")—objectionable, because theology teaches us that God uses men to achieve His ends.

It is, however, quite frequently forgotten that the essential question still remains unanswered. An axiom of Catholic moral teaching is *agere sequitur esse*, "duty follows being." The original point of departure was always that God created the world at the beginning of time and that His creation was "good" (Gen. 1. 25). Every change had to make this creation less good, and since it was not possible for God to botch up His own world, evolution could only be assumed to have come from the devil. Pastor Süssmilch, however, saw the "divine order" in these "changes."

The question which believers ask those who believe in progress, then, is this: Are the natural changes that have taken place in the evolution of living organisms apart from man, or even all the social changes that have been brought about by man, sanctioned by the will of God? If they are, then God's will is a concept that man can dispense with and the Ten Commandments can be replaced by ten descriptions. If they are not, then all that remains is for man to admit that changes will also take place, as man and human society evolve in the course of further history, in the moral demands that follow man's "being." We also have to recognize in this case that these demands must be orientated towards this possibility, although they are not identical. The comment of a theologian in this context is that "the moral norm which applies to man must change in every case to exactly the same degree that man's being changes in history."[56] He does not say, however, where this norm comes from.

Comte and his fellow scientists of the eighteenth and early nineteenth centuries, who strike us in many ways as so modern, are remarkable in that, although they used the methods of natural science in their study of man, they applied them exclusively to man, never to the animal kingdom. Their interest was confined to human biology and sociology and they analyzed man himself. They did not draw as many conclusions as possible from experiments with and observations of animals and then apply these to man, nor did they even look first in the animal world for parallels with man. The really striking aspect of biological and sociological research is that it was carried out directly with man.

The question of parallels is, however, an important one and I shall discuss it now and later try to ascertain how they can help us find ethical norms.

It has frequently been suggested that differences in social behavior and in social systems are not purely fortuitous, but are ultimately dependent on environmental factors. In 1878, the French philosopher, economist and historian A. Espinas[13] published a book on animal societies in which he, unlike so many research workers before him, looked for parallels with human social patterns in the animal kingdom, drawing extensively on Brehm's "Animal Life" for his material. He made several important discoveries. The first was that animal societies almost always consisted of individuals of the same species. He also found that closely related species often had very different social systems, whereas almost identical social systems could appear in quite different, almost totally unrelated species. He concluded from this evidence that similarities in the social systems of animals were more a question of convergence than of homology, and consequently set out to investigate which ecological conditions produced which forms of animal society.

In 1905, the Belgian sociologist Raphael Petrucci decided that it was useless to try to correlate the complexity of the social life of a species with its intelligence and a year later came to the same conclusion as Espinas, that is, that the social system was produced by the needs of the species' environment.

Nowadays, we are in possession of excellent examples

demonstrating this dependence on the environment. We know that the same species can have different social systems according to the conditions imposed by its environment.[73] The wren, for example, is generally monogamous when it lives in an environment where it has to exert itself to find food, and the cock and the hen feed and raise the young together in such circumstances. Where there is more than enough to eat, on the other hand, each male bird has several wives, each one with a nest and each one feeding and raising the young birds without the help of the male. Great antelopes, such as those investigated between 1962 and 1965 by Estes[14] (the African gnu or wildebeest), live nomadically in great herds, with groups of bachelor gnus joined to them, when they are in dry territories. Whereas they only have occasional temporary preserves when food and water is scarce, then, they become sedentary in districts where there is enough to eat and drink, the mates forming permanent preserves which border on each other. The herds of bachelors keep away both from these and from the small herds of mothers and their young, which also confine themselves to one place.

The method that is followed, then, is to compare as many animals as possible that are living monogamously in a small group. We do this in order to learn just how closely the social system is correlated to the environmental situation. We also hope, in carrying out this sort of experiment, to be able to predict with some certainty which social system we can expect to find under which circumstances, no matter which animal we are dealing with.

The hope that it may be possible to make this forecast is based on our biological knowledge that the behavior of a living organism is, as it were, its most flexible and easily molded organ and that it is above all this variable behavior which makes possible survival and the exploitation of life's

53

possibilities under varying circumstances of life and environmental conditions.

This view has for a long time been closely connected with the science of "ethology." There has long been a branch of scientific research with this name and it was Isidore G. Saint-Hilaire who, in 1854, applied, within the larger framework of biology, the concept of "ethology" to what Ernst Haeckel in 1866 called "ecology." Later still, at the turn of the century, the Belgian palaeontologist Louis Dollo did research, under the name of "ethology," into the behavioral adaptability of living organisms to their environment. This "ethological and phylogenetical" method was used until very recently to analyze various types of animal life in phylogenetical research.[69] What is more, it is undeniably true to say that this view, namely that organisms adapt themselves to their environment, was handed down by the earlier ecological ethologists to the later ethologists, who then called their science "modern" ethology, to distinguish it from these earlier movements.

As early as 1906, the Belgian scientist Émile Waxweiler[66] constructed, on the basis of this older form of ecological ethology, an imposing research project which was unfortunately never completed because of the First World War. He began with a theory of comparison and hoped, by extensive experimentation, to make a close-knit synthesis of animal and human social ethology. In Waxweiler's plan, sociology figured as a special branch of ethology concerned with the phenomena arising from man's particular social abilities. His aim was to investigate the universally valid biological principles of social behavior by comparing suitable animal societies. Today we are looking once again to see if biology can help us in any way to find answers to the many open social and ethical questions raised by ethological research. It is possible to look for the answers in those

54

spheres which provide us with information about analogous moral behavior in animals.

In 1954, Konrad Lorenz published an article entitled "Analogous Moral Behavior in Social Animals"[35] in which he drew attention to the behavior of "armed" animals. Animals possessing, in other words, powerful teeth, horns or stings, with which they are able to kill other members of the same species, regularly have certain behavioral mechanisms which prevent them from doing so. The moral of this is, of course, that man ought to think of some process, whenever he has dangerous weapons at his disposal, which would prevent him from murdering his fellow men.

Lorenz also gives an analogy from the animal kingdom for our moral demand that weaker individuals should be helped. An order of rank corresponding to the degree of strength of the individual members automatically establishes itself among animals living in groups. A good example of this is what happens in a colony of jackdaws. As soon as a quarrel breaks out between two birds, the jackdaw that occupies the highest rank in the colony at once intervenes in favor of the one that is lowest in rank, the weakest member. This is not done out of a feeling of compassion, of course, but simply because every jackdaw is more aggressive in its attitude towards others that are closer to it in rank and strength than towards those that are further away and weaker. Whenever a jackdaw intervenes in a fight, then, it will inevitably attack the stronger bird that is close to it in rank. Its help of the weaker bird is therefore indirect.

As long ago as 1880, the zoologist Professor Kessler asserted at a congress of Russian natural scientists that the continuing evolution of species in the animal kingdom was promoted not only by the struggle for existence that Darwin had so rightly stressed, but also by a "law of mutual aid."

55

Kessler believed that "parental feeling" and care for offspring were the two main sources of mutual affection between animals. I shall be returning to this question later, in my chapter on sexual partnership (see p. 124). Kessler's idea was taken further by Prince Peter Kropotkin,[28] who is best known as the most important representative of communist anarchism, in a book entitled *Mutual Aid in Evolution,* which he published in 1904. Many of the examples which he used to illustrate his thesis would be interpreted differently today.

It would seem as though animals cannot deviate from this analogous moral behavior, whereas human beings know that they are able to act immorally. Lorenz's theory was expressed more than four hundred years ago by Sebastian Franck in the collection of proverbs that he translated from ancient Latin hexameters into simple verse:

> When did a serpent ever take
> The life of another fellow snake?
> Never in nature do we find
> That lion or bear kills its own kind.
> Boars are at peace with other boars,
> No tiger tears tiger in its jaws.
> Man is not so—the blood he spills
> Is that of the men he wounds and kills.

In these naïve lines, man is compared with animals and their behavior is implicitly placed on the same level. We are bound to ask, then, whether analogous moral behavior may perhaps be entirely lacking in man. His behavior would be analogously moral if he were to behave unreflectingly, but only if this spontaneous action were to turn out as though it had been previously thought out, in other words, if it were to pass a subsequent test of morality.

The problem, however variously it has been formulated, has preoccupied leading thinkers for a long time. Schiller, for example, expressed it with classical irony in the lines that he headed "Scruples of Conscience": "I like to serve my friends, but unfortunately I have a natural propensity to do so; I am therefore often annoyed because I am not virtuous." His solution to this problem was: "You have no other choice. You must learn to despise them and do your duty with loathing."

The categorical imperative of Kant, who insisted that doing one's duty was a necessary aspect of ethical behavior, can in this way be reduced to absurdity and the falsity of the contrast between doing one's duty and natural propensity can be easily enough exposed. It would seem that this misleading contrast is closely connected with the widespread view that man is either diametrically opposed to nature or else superior to it, at the very least that he does not belong to nature. Even our knowledge that this is not true can hardly save us from a vague feeling that a good action may not be entirely valueless, but certainly has less value if it is motivated by nature and not by a sense of duty.

Even today, there are scientists who are unaware of Schiller's irony and are earnestly convinced that it is only possible to love one's neighbor if one goes contrary to one's natural inclinations, with the result that they insist that "it is not an ethical act to help one's friends."[23] It would seem as though man is capable of analogous moral behavior, but that he regards it as beneath his dignity to take advantage of this ability. This inevitably leads to the attitude that all man's natural impulses come from the devil, especially when they are pleasurable. Such a drastic way of expressing this attitude may strike some as unacceptable, but it cannot be denied on the other hand that reprehensible actions can hardly be excused on the grounds that they are the result of natural propensities. How can this problem be solved without the use of irony?

We regard man as the most highly developed living organism on earth. This is not simply pride; there is a norm, according to which the development of all organisms can be graded as higher or as less high. This norm has nothing to do with phylogenetic age, that is to say, it does not mean that because a species has arisen later in the history of the evolution of organisms, it will automatically occupy a higher position on the scale of development than a species which preceded it in the chronology of evolution. The norm that we apply in this case is rather the mass of information about the world and its immediate environment that a living organism can gather, store and use. Parasites, which have dispensed with whole organs which their ancestors possessed and can therefore acquire fewer data about their environment, are good examples of organisms that have evolved backwards. Although they have appeared more recently in the history of evolution, they are not higher organisms.

The higher the development of the organism and the more data it can collect concerning its environment, the less firmly it is established. If this were not so, it would not be able to adapt its behavior to the situation or make use of its experience. This is particularly true for man: he is able to differentiate between a greater variety of situations than has been programed in his intuitive biological pattern of behavior, for which solutions have been previously provided. If there is no ready solution, however, man has to decide how he should act and, if he has a natural propensity to behave in a certain way, he must still decide whether or not he should follow this inclination. This means that he has to use his reason. If we regard this as a characteristically human possibility, we shall judge man's actions according to whether they have been taken after human reason has been consulted. This confronts us, however, with a techni-

58

cal difficulty—one which is perhaps not entirely unexpected —and here lies the root of our problem: how can we tell when man is acting rationally?

There is at least one deceptively easy answer to this question. If the natural propensity is known and someone acts in contradiction to it, as the good Samaritan did in showing neighborly love to his enemy, we may say with a high degree of probability that he has considered this action rationally in advance. If, on the other hand, he acts according to his natural propensity and helps his friend, he may or may not have consulted human reason beforehand. Since it is never possible to know exactly whether this is so or not, a certain imbalance creeps into our assessment of our actions. This tends to make us think that we are acting virtuously if we go against our natural inclinations, which we think of as base and even bestial. We therefore tend to regard actions which are contrary to our natural inclinations as especially meritorious because they show particularly clearly that human reason has been consulted beforehand, not because they were contrary to our inclinations.

It is no less meritorious to act when reason urges us to follow a natural propensity. Anyone who believes that this will never happen clearly supposes that man has been wrongly constructed by nature, so wrongly in fact that, if he wants to act well, he has constantly to go against the way in which he has been naturally constructed. This is unintelligible both from the biological and from the theological point of view.

We can now attempt to answer Schiller's question. It is man's duty critically to examine his own inclinations to act well, but it is not necessarily virtuous to act contrary to them. To express this idea in a different way, analogous moral behavior in man does not become relevant moral behavior simply by preceding it with a negative sign. It does so above all if it is preceded by an ethical sign, which may at the same time also be positive. This is in any case precisely what we might expect, because we know from our own experience that human "common sense" is as dependent on "instinctive" good behavior as it is on the Kantian categorical imperative. Even in our choice of friends, we tend to prefer people whose friendly behavior is the result not simply of rational reflection, but also of natural inclination and affection. We associate more willingly with people who act in a friendly way towards us because they are prompted by a natural propensity than with those who feel obliged to hold themselves constantly in check in everyday life because of a sense of moral responsibility.

An example that is frequently given to illustrate the positive value of instinctive action is that of a child falling into the water. Anyone seeing this happen is expected to jump in after the child without reflecting. It is even possible to lay the blame on rational reflection for this, because, if the man who saw the child fall into the water were to consider the whole question carefully before jumping in, the child would probably drown in the meantime. Even though it would undoubtedly be less effective, would this delayed attempt to save the child be any less meritorious?

Are natural inclinations in themselves ethically good rather than bad? I do not think so. All that the example of the child falling into the water shows us is that it may be correct to follow a natural propensity without reflecting. It does not show that unreflecting action is in itself good or correct. The haste that is a feature of this particular case conceals the difference, but, in different circumstances, this very haste can have very bad consequences. A classic example of this is the tragic situation of the "hero" who, from a natural inclination to save his friend from danger, shoots or does something similar without reflection and without

60

taking stock of the situation. Had he done so, he would have known that his impulsive action would endanger his friend even more and perhaps even lead to his death.

There are, of course, many situations in which a very quick decision has to be made and there is neither the time nor the opportunity to reflect fully about the imminent action that has to be taken. In cases such as this, we have need of norms or guidelines which we can use to make our decision easier. I do not in any sense want to advocate unreflecting action or discredit the habit of reflecting before acting, simply because it takes time. We should certainly reflect whenever we have time to do so. We should not reflect when time is pressing and we are in an emergency. After all, it is as the result of mature reflection that we find, or should find our guidelines for making decisions. Thought out in tranquillity, they assume the form of carefully considered commandments, like those which I have already quoted. These guidelines must of necessity be kept general rather than specific, so that they can be applied to a wide variety of cases. They will therefore be formulated as apodeictic commandments, which begin with "you shall . . ." and state the intention of the commandment, rather than describe casuistically individual instances and their consequences. The form "if someone does this or that, then . . ." will, in other words, be avoided. A collection of specific cases expressed in this way would be historically interesting, but would have little ethical value. To be sure, casuistry of the kind outlined above is of interest to the biologist. As we have seen, he describes and compares the behavior of as many species of animal as possible and tries to define the analogous moral laws that underlie this behavior. He also attempts to do the same with human behavior. If he knows in advance how moral commandments applying generally to many different cases are formulated, he can learn from individual cases how to interpret the general directives contained in these commandments. What emerges, then, is that, in the case of higher animals, the relationship that exists between parent animals, for example, is so arranged according to the norms of analogous moral behavior that interference from outsiders into this relationship between the parents is effectively prevented. What also emerges, however, is that this arrangement differs from species to species and even within the same species according to circumstances.

This is very similar to the human situation in which adultery is generally regarded as tabu. The norm governing adultery can, however, as in the case of higher animals, also differ from one group of people to another and even within the same people according to circumstances. It depends, in other words, on whether the people in question practice monogamy, polygyny or polyandry.

Advanced research into animal societies has revealed that there are certain sensitive areas in the social life of animals which occur again and again in many different species. These can be summarized under five headings.

1. The handing down of traditions, authority—attentiveness to old members of the society.

2. The killing of members of the same species.

3. Sexual relationships between partners.

4. Possession and ownership.

5. Reliable, "true" communication.

It is impossible to ignore the fact that these delicate zones in animal societies are also covered by our commandments. The social behavior of animals is governed by commandments, and one of the tasks of ethology is to discover the physiological and other biological laws of this analogous moral behavior.

Human Ecological Ethology
—Who Is Our Neighbor?

THE seven commandments that are directly related to our fellow men can, of course, be summarized under one heading: you shall love your neighbor as yourself. The difficulties that arise in this connection are also based on biological laws and, here too, there are parallels with the animal kingdom. It might be possible to speak in this context of analogous amoral behavior, and this is something that I should like to discuss, because it illustrates one form of the dependence of man's social behavior on his environment.

Closely related species make more or less the same demands on their environment. They require, for example, the same food and the same nesting or sleeping places. They would thus be in close competition with each other if they lived in close proximity. They can, in fact, only do this if they avoid each other by specializing in different spheres of activity. (An illustration of this type of behavior is activity at different times of day or night.) They form, in other words, different ecological niches. The more closely related they are to each other, the more easily they can interbreed. When this happens, their areas of specialization become merged and the differences between their behavior cease to exist.

Two species can continue to exist side by side only when they avoid hybridization. This regularly leads to mechanisms which prevent crossbreeding arising in precisely those spheres in which hybrids might occur. Species which come together only in a small area of their total geographical distribution often differ more sharply from each other where they coincide geographically than where only one of the species occurs and there is consequently no danger of interbreeding. This emphasizing of contrasts between species occurs, for example, in the case of many closely related American toads. The mating calls of the males differ markedly in areas where two species overlap, but can hardly be distinguished from each other when the areas of distribution are separate.

This same tendency to stress contrasts can also be observed in man. What is more, the characteristics which are emphasized do not have to be innate. An example will perhaps make it clear how this phenomenon is connected with ecological factors and is therefore biologically meaningful. The Australian aborigines live in tribal groups which are characterized by several distinctive features. Firstly, each group inhabits and "owns" a definite territory. Secondly, the members of each group have their own language or dialect. Thirdly, they have customs and laws which are to some extent different from those of neighboring groups. These people have always been collectors and hunters, spending the entire day with the whole of their family looking for food and managing to survive in the most desolate and least hospitable regions. Professor Elkin[12] of Sydney University has studied these aboriginal tribes for many years. One of the most interesting discoveries that he has made is that each tribe distinguishes five to seven seasons, usually of different length, and calls them by names which clearly indicate the prevailing weather and the best food obtainable.

Thus, the inhabitants of Arnhem Land near Maranboy have the following seasons: (1) June–July, Honey; (2) August–October, Late Dry Period; (3) November–December, First Rains, First Fruit; (4) January–March, Rainy Period, Yam Roots; (5) April, Game; May, Cool West

Winds. For the people of the Swan River in Western Australia, the seasons are: (1) June–July, Yetta Roots; (2) August–October, Orchid Roots; (3) October–November, Young Birds; (4) December–January, Lizards, Bronze-winged Pigeons; (5) February–March, Mullet, Trout; (6) April–May, Reed Roots, Frogs buried in the Sand.

What food has to be looked for and at what period depends on when the rainy and the dry seasons occur in the region in question and whether the region is situated on the coast, on the bank of a river or on the dry plain. In the hottest season of the year, the Bard people who live on a peninsula in Arnhem Land catch turtles, whereas the Karadjeri who live two hundred miles to the west near La Grange in Kimberley catch kangaroos. In April, there is a great deal of game in the region of Maranboy and reed roots and frogs abound near the Swan River.

What has to be looked for (and when) is something that every member of the tribe has to learn from the older, more experienced members. His life depends on whether he learns this and the lives of his children depend on whether he teaches them properly. If a Bard were to hunt kangaroos in Arnhem Land, following the example of the Karadjeri in Kimberley, he would probably starve to death. But he would never even attempt to catch kangaroos, and would regard any Karadjeri who tried to persuade him to do so as mad.

As a general rule, every tribe suspects its neighbors of practicing deceit because they talk such obvious nonsense when discussing important everyday questions. Neighboring tribes do in fact regularly accuse each other of harboring cunning plans and deceitful intentions. Listening to one's neighbors is not simply superfluous—it can also be dangerous. A tribe protects itself against such dangerous influences by not exchanging information. Although the Australian tribes understand each others' languages and can

65

speak with their neighbors, they do not do so, and in fact avoid all contact with each other.

What we have, then, in the case of these tribes, each of which is intent on adapting itself to its own ecological conditions, is the phenomenon of accentuation of contrasts in those areas where two closely related groups overlap. This prevents the process of adaptation from being disturbed. Each tribe accentuates its particular tradition, rites and customs and has hardly anything good to say of its neighbors. Many groups go so far as to accuse their neighbors of cannibalism. Research workers have been astonished to find nothing of the kind practiced by the neighboring tribe when they have visited it. But they have been equally surprised to hear the group they have just left accused of the same practice.

The Dutch ethnologist, Professor Oosterwal, had this to say about the Papuas of New Guinea. "While I was making preparations for the long journey, the village people came to me and said: 'Nana, why are you going away? Stay here. Don't go to the Waf and the Daranto and the Mander and the Foja. The Waf are dirty and stupid. They are bad people. The Daranto are wicked. You can't trust them. We don't know the Foja, but we have heard that they are savage and cruel.' I had been told things like this before by the Bora-Bora, but now, just before my departure, they repeated them so emphatically that I involuntarily believed them. They all said these things, even Djiri and the old Sama, both of whom were so impartial in their judgment.

"I was prepared for the worst, but when I reached the Waf, I was welcomed by the men of the tribe, who gave me a huge piece of roasted pork as a gift. Later, I arrived at the territory of the Foja and they proved to be as friendly, as hospitable and as helpful as the others. There was no sign of cruelty and they were no dirtier or more stupid than the other tribes. What is very remarkable, however, is that the

66

Waf asked me: 'Nana, were you afraid when you were with the Bora-Bora?' I looked at them in astonishment. I cannot imagine any more friendly people than the Bora-Bora. 'Afraid?' I asked. 'But why?' The Waf looked at me seriously, discussed the matter among themselves and then turned back to me. 'Nana,' they said, 'we know that the Bora-Bora are stupid, cruel people.'

"A week later, I was with the Mander, who told me at great length how inferior the Waf and the Daranto were. In the evening, round the fire of blazing logs, we talked with each other and the conversation always returned to the same theme—the excellence of the Mander themselves and the dirtiness, stupidity and cruelty of the other tribes. The children in the villages heard these stories day after day, and they must have grown up convinced that the Waf and the Daranto were lazy and stupid and that the Segar and the Baguidja were feeble-minded and cruel. This played a decisive part in the children's future attitude towards the other tribes. The less contact these people had with each other, the more excellent they thought themselves to be. The greater their isolation from the other tribes, the more negative was their judgment of them. It is the same everywhere in the world."[48]

As long as people lack understanding of the biological, ecological and ethological relationships that exist between themselves and "others"—however these others are defined —they will inevitably continue to defame them in order to defend and protect themselves. The easier it is to avoid competitive contact with the other members of one's own species and the more spheres there are in which one can specialize, the more groups there must be with which one has to be contrasted. The more sharply one group distinguishes itself from others by accentuating this contrast, the more safely it can remain within its own area of specialization and the more securely it can be protected from disturbing influences. At the same time, however, it also runs the serious risk of regarding other groups of the same species with different zones of specialization as alien, of treating them as such and eventually of coming into open conflict with them. It is this very same process that also leads to the emergence of new species. Man is probably, of all living organisms, the one with the greatest propensity for specialization and differentiation, and is thus likely to be the species with the greatest tendency to group hatred.

Sociologists recognize that isolation from influences that are alien to the group actively promotes integration on the part of the group. "As soon as the individual has learnt the parts that he has to play in the group," Seger insists, "he is concerned to protect his knowledge. In other words, he does not want it to be disturbed by ideas that contradict it . . . The stronger the feeling of group egoism becomes, the more the group mistrusts or despises other groups. Despite all assurances to the contrary, national pride is always accompanied by a devaluation of other nationalities, racial pride always leads to contempt of other races, and solidarity among retail traders or factory workers always results in suspicion of other groups . . . The practice of having special names for one's own group and for other groups and a distinctive jargon or slang terminology forms an essential part of the mechanism used by each group to reinforce its inner solidarity and its isolation from other groups. Criminals have their own language; so also do scientists, young people, anarchists and the initiates of all religions."[57]

Groups certainly find their own special niches not only in their purely climatic and topographical environment, but also in their wider social environment. This phenomenon is always clearly revealed in their speech. Language influences thought, however, because it is not just a collection of useful names and phrases—it also reflects and even fashions categories of thought. The worker-priest experiment in

France was terminated by the Vatican because the priests were beginning to think like their companions at work and after work.

Every group, of course, regards its own norms simply as "moral," even though they may be restricted to the group's own environment, and forms prejudgments—which can easily stand in the way of real judgments—in order to protect itself against the rules of other groups. As Charles de Montesquieu wrote in 1748 in his well-known work of political philosophy, *De l'esprit des lois:* "In the northern zones, we meet people with few vices, sufficient virtues and a great deal of honesty and openness. As we approach the countries of the south, however, we have the impression that we are leaving morality behind us." It should be noted that Montesquieu was himself an inhabitant of the northern zones.

This initially unconscious tendency can be contrasted with the commandment to love our neighbor. According to this precept, every member of the same species is our neighbor. What is most important is that it can only be followed consciously and is in direct opposition to the unconscious tendency to stress differences between groups of the same species. There are, of course, both positive possibilities for and difficulties in following this commandment, from the purely human point of view. There are, however, also purely biological aids and obstacles and I should like to examine these more closely in the following chapters. In all the groups that are known to me, no matter how they originated, I have observed one common factor. This is a constant contrast between a tendency on the part of each group to specialize and to isolate itself from other groups and an opposite tendency to regard all men as brothers. Even the apostle Paul said, after all, that Christians as a group should do good to all men, but especially to fellow believers.

Digression
—What Does "Social" Mean?

THE word "social" that I have used so much in the preceding chapters, together with related terms such as "society," "sociology," "social behavior" and so on, may have caused a certain unease in the minds of some readers. Others may simply have accepted these terms unquestioningly, even though their meaning has not been made absolutely clear. They can, of course, mean different things, according to the branch of research in which they are used.

A botanist can practice plant sociology, in which case his main interest is in plant societies. A plant society includes everything that grows in a particular place. In this instance, then, the term "society" stresses the occurrence together in the same place of different species of plants. Plant sociology therefore is the study of relationships between different species.

The biologist who specializes in animal sociology, on the other hand, studies the relationships between members of the same species, because animal societies—as Espinas pointed out in the nineteenth century[13]—regularly consist of individuals of the same species. This is obviously connected with the fact that animals are fairly mobile and can select their neighbors.

"Sociology" without any explanatory or descriptive noun or adjective is also concerned with groups consisting of individuals of the same species, in this case, however, of only one species—man. Social relationships do not occur as a theme in the study of plant societies and they are only discussed in the animal kingdom when animals are able to move around independently of other animals belonging to the same species. Anthozoa such as corals and bryozoa, for example, behave like plants and seem to have no social life as such.

In this context, it should also be noted that, in German scientific circles, the term "social relationships" is applied above all to those between the same species, whereas in England and America, every kind of relationship which includes more than one individual is called "social." Although research into social relationships between members of the same species predominates in the English-speaking world, it can also deal with relationships between individuals of different species.

Similarly, "social behavior" is used by German-speaking ethologists and others to denote all behavior that is beneficial to all concerned, but is generally restricted to members of the same species. Among English-speaking specialists, on the other hand, the term is often applied to behavior between partners of different species, in other words, to symbiotic behavior.

There is social behavior in all species of animals, whenever those species engage in mating displays directed towards a female of the same species, fight as rivals or have some form of relationship between parents and offspring.

Social animals as such, on the other hand, are creatures leading lives in which social behavior predominates. They are, in other words, animals which form societies. Well-known examples of such societies are, of course, shoals of fish, communities of insects and permanent family groups of certain kinds of apes.

It does occasionally happen in ethological research that

71

the term "social behavior" gives rise to confusion and mis-understanding, because the opposite to "social" is involun-tarily called to mind. This may be "nonsocial" or "asocial." The first is neutral and, in ethology, simply denotes be-havior that is not related to members of the same species. In the sphere of human sociology, however, "social" gen-erally has the connotation of being consciously oriented toward the advancement and welfare of one's fellow men. In fact, it has such distinct moral overtones that purely instinctive "analogous moral" behavior directed towards one's fellow men, of the kind investigated by ethologists and regarded by them as social behavior, tends not to be re-garded as such in the human sphere.

This is a cause of misunderstanding between ethologists and sociologists, between animal sociologists and human sociologists. The term "unsocial" or "asocial," however, does not point to the absence of a social relationship on the part of the active animal (or human being). What it does emphasize are the harmful effects of this activity on others or on the society as a whole. What is known as "unsocial" can, in fact, usually be called "antisocial." (On the other hand, what is known as antiauthoritarian education or up-bringing ought properly to be called "unauthoritarian" up-bringing. Bad word formations often prove to be very hard to dislodge, however.)

This kind of terminological confusion is probably in-evitable. It would be futile, after all, to pretend that all branches of science speak the same language.

PART 2

Aggression Between Members of the Same Species
—You Shall Not Kill

THE Fifth Commandment, "You shall not kill," is one of the earliest of the ethical precepts and yet the one which is most discussed nowadays. The central theme of the debate, however, is not the principle expressed in the commandment, but the exceptional cases that are usually included under this heading—killing in war and in self-defense, the death penalty, euthanasia, abortion and suicide.

What is particularly striking in the formulation of this commandment in the Decalogue, however, is that a special verb is used for "kill," a verb that is never used elsewhere in the Bible for killing an opponent in war or for the execution of someone condemned to death. It is only employed for the killing or murdering of a personal opponent. Ancient Israel was familiar with the death penalty and war (even war that was forbidden by God!) and even blood revenge was legitimate (and still is in Jordan). The commandment, then, is directed against unbounded, illegal killing. Even vengeance ought to take place legally: "Life for life, eye for eye, tooth for tooth, hand for hand, foot for foot, burn for burn, wound for wound, stripe for stripe" (Exodus 21. 23ff.).

"It is remarkable, however," Kropotkin has observed, "that in the case of a sentence of death, nobody will take upon himself to be the executioner. Every one throws his

75

stone or gives his blow with the hatchet, carefully avoiding to give a mortal blow. At a later epoch, the priest will stab the victim with a sacred knife. Still later, it will be the king, until civilization invents the hired hangman . . . A remainder of this tribal habit . . . has survived in military executions till our own times" (Kropotkin was writing at the beginning of this century). "In the middle portion of the nineteenth century, it was the habit to load the rifles of the twelve soldiers called out for shooting the condemned victim with eleven ball-cartridges and one blank cartridge. As the soldiers never knew who of them had the latter, each one could console his disturbed conscience by thinking that he was not one of the murderers."[28]

Man's conscience, then, cannot be indifferent to the act of killing a fellow man, even when this is legally sanctioned. The man who murders because it is his duty to do so seeks refuge in the indiscriminate mass of mankind, and the individual would rather persecute a fellow man over a long period than kill him quickly.

All this points clearly enough to the existence of an inhibition against killing in man, although it is not possible to infer from the evidence that this inhibition is instinctive. If, however, we were to find an instinctive inhibition against killing among animals generally, then we might expect man to have preserved some remnants at least of this inhibition, in other words, that it was not eliminated altogether in the process of becoming man.

Obviously, it is to be hoped that the biologist might help the theologian here, because the commandment not to kill is quite clearly related to the natural law and to the laws of preservation of the species. It has, moreover, never been questioned that this commandment forbids the killing of members of the same species, which, in this case, are one's fellow men. What is more, an "emotional" dividing line is often drawn between fellow men who are anonymous and those whom we know, in which case animals—creatures that are not human—certainly cannot be included within this commandment, although an exception may have to be made with regard to totem animals and organisms that are closely connected with man.

The obvious course, then, is to accept the biologist's fundamental law of preservation of the species as a basis for argument. Any killing of a member of the same species is contrary to this law and is therefore bound, as a general rule, to be unbiological. The great success of Konrad Lorenz's book *On Aggression*[36] was primarily due to the fact that he used this extremely plausible argument: living organisms that are capable of killing other creatures of the same size as themselves have to develop special mechanisms to prevent them from behaving in the same way with rivals of the same species and thereby exterminating themselves. "The suitability of and indeed the need for this kind of inhibiting mechanism so that the species will be preserved is as obvious as the unsuitability of and the need to avoid the killing of other members of the same species," Lorenz insisted.

In considering the whole question, however, it will be found useful to develop something of an allergy to the word "obvious." Above all, we need to try to discover what lies behind basic laws which sound like commonplaces. Three terms in particular occur very frequently in this context and it is important to understand what they mean. They are "evil," "aggression" and "member of the same species."

1. *Can the biologist do anything with the concept of "Evil"?* In principle, he cannot. He can certainly distinguish

between correct and wrong modes of behavior by measuring and checking them to determine whether they are beneficial or harmful to the survival of the individual or the species. He cannot, on the other hand, assess them ethically as good or evil, because these moral categories lie beyond the scope of the knowledge acquired by modern scientific methods. The natural scientist can, however, try to find explanations for the causes of modes of behavior, which may then be called good or evil by the moral theologian. The question as to how far the biological antithesis of correct and wrong should agree with the ethical polarity of good and evil can only be answered by the biologist and the theologian working in close cooperation. (It should be noted that the methods used by theologians to find ethical norms have not yet been fully elaborated, and this stands in the way of full collaboration between the two sides. This difficulty is increased by the fact that biologists are very critical with regard to these norms, whereas theologians are at present mainly concerned with criticizing methodology. This means that the most profitable form of cooperation between the two at this point will not be simply to criticize conclusions, but rather to reveal parallels between ethology and ethics.)

If the killing of members of the same species is called evil and is attributed to aggression, all that the natural scientist can do is to look for causes for such evil aggression. To carry out this task, the biologist, and above all the zoologist, is confronted at once with a special method that he uses to investigate "disturbing characteristics," that is, those which yield no biological sense or meaning. For instance, the cave fish that live in continuous darkness do have eyes, but eyes without lenses, or eyes that are so deformed that even if there were light in the caves, the fish would see nothing. What use, then, are the eyes of these fish? Why do they have eyes at all? Why do we have an appendix? Why does the young whale develop teeth, which he loses again before birth? In all these and similar questions, there is an assumption that the organism is adapted to its environmental needs, that the structure is in accordance with the performance required, and that any incongruence between the structure and the performance is bound to cause surprise and therefore calls for a special explanation.

It is possible for anyone who is spurred on by an ideal of creation to carry these questions quite a long way. He may wonder at the structure of the human eye, for instance, and be convinced that it is impossible to explain the way in which it has come about simply by natural means. If so, as soon as he examines the structure of the eye more closely, he is bound to ask why it is that the cells that are sensitive to light in the retina point away from the light, as though the film had been placed in a camera with the reverse side facing forward. Since he may have an ideal mental image of the structure of the eye or of any other part of the body, he will want to find explanations for all the deviations from this ideal. This will, of course, provide him with an abundant source of questions.

He need not abandon his basic assumption that the organism is already fully adapted. He will, however, probably find the answer to his questions in the history of evolution. As far as certain characteristics are concerned, many organisms are either not yet fully adapted or else no longer adapted. This is quite plausible, and is in fact completely in accordance with the experience of many animal breeders. No organism changes suddenly, nor do all the parts of its body change at the same time. Chickens have two legs, feathers and a tail, but their color, size and laying performance change. This takes time. A captive Red Jungle Fowl will not produce as many eggs as a Leghorn hen, nor will its young. The Red Jungle Fowl is not yet adapted to the demands that we make of the domestic chicken. The reverse is true of the Leghorn hen, which as a domestic chicken is not equal to the demands of the jungle.

In the same way, Lorenz has explained human aggression, which we nowadays regard as disturbing, as a "historical encumbrance." He sees it as a quality which was of use to man in the earliest period of his history, when he lived in nomadic hordes in rivalry with other groups. Although man still has this aggressive characteristic, Lorenz recognizes that it no longer fits into the modern settled way of life in heavily populated areas.

Aggression, then, is one of the peculiarities which man has derived from the prehistoric phase of his existence. The presence of these qualities in modern man shows that he is not yet "good" enough. This means, of course, that he is not yet sufficiently adapted. But the biologist can include these qualities among Lorenz's "so-called evil" elements and one of them clearly is, as we have seen, aggression. A prior condition for the inclusion of any quality is that it be, as it were, impossible to lose it. It may either be directly rooted in man's heredity ("innate"), or continually emerge as a by-product of the contemporary form of the influence of society on the individual during his development, in which case it may have been inherited from prehistoric times.

Generally speaking, it is not aggression itself that is regarded as evil, but exaggerated aggressiveness. Most people believe, even today, that some aggression, some spirit of rivalry, some self-assertion and determination to succeed are necessary. The origin of historical ballast of this kind has still to be investigated, but we can safely say that it is the aggregate of aggression which is still present and is very difficult to reduce. Various research workers in this sphere who subscribe to a definite view of instinctive behavior suspect that there is an aggression energy which is automatically produced in a characteristic aggregate. This will be discussed more fully on p. 100. In the meantime, several other, more urgent questions have to be answered.

2. *What is a member of the same species?* A species is the totality of natural populations forming together an exclusive reproductive community. Members of these populations beget offspring, under natural conditions, only with each other and not with members of other population groups. Since, however, not every individual in fact ever begets offspring with every other individual of the opposite sex, but only with a few members of that sex and of the right age-group, what is strictly speaking meant in this definition of species is the potential reproductive community.

A very extensive survey is needed to determine which are in fact the individuals forming a potential reproductive community. In 1935, Lorenz[34] emphasized that only mankind can be surveyed and classified in this way because, as far as animals are concerned, there are no members of the same species in the sense of "companions." An animal finds one partner or companion for fighting, another for mating and another for care of the young. Lorenz called these partners the fighting companion, the mating companion, the companion for raising the young and so on. He argued that since members of the same species in the animal world were subdivided into so many different social companions, a general inhibition against killing a member of the same species could hardly be expected to exist.

In fact, different inhibitions exist in the animal kingdom preventing the killing of the fighting partner, the mating partner or the young. Not all these inhibitions, however,

81

are present in one and the same individual. For example, certain fish that do not share in looking after the young fight each other according to special rules and regulations prohibiting the killing of the weaker partner. These males, however, also eat their own young if they happen to encounter them. Members of the same species which are sick or which behave, for one reason or another, in an unusual way can be attacked as if they were of a different species and even killed. In the case of species which fight according to special "rules," injury or death often comes to the individual that does not keep to these rules.

I have already drawn attention elsewhere to the fact that species that fight according to special rules are also capable of fighting to inflict injury. Among members of the same species who are not capable of this, the first individual who was able to would win at once, conquering all its rivals and thus introducing—or re-introducing—fighting for the purpose of inflicting injury.[69] *Aequalitas non parit bellum*—equality does not lead to war. An arms race between rivals, each of which is anxious to survive, can also be justified biologically on the grounds that each may be able to hope in the maintenance of peace. Of course, there are also fights which do not result in death or injury because neither of the partners possesses organs which can be used as dangerous weapons. Such species do regularly engage in combats, but these can hardly be called duels fought according to specialized rules. This concept has, strictly speaking, to be reserved exclusively for the duels fought between species that also fight in order to injure each other.

A species' knowledge of its social partner is, however, not always innate. It can also be and often is acquired. It is possible, for example, for a brood parasite to get to know its foster parents as social companions even though they belong to a different species. On the other hand, different groups of the same species are distinguished by their group characteristics and when these characteristics of the social partner are acquired, representatives of different groups are treated as members of a different species. A bee which gets into a hive that is not its own is killed because it has the "wrong" hive smell. Thus an organism may look on others of the same species as different, not only because they have different ecological adaptations, but also because they have different group characteristics.

In many species, only the males, not the females, fight according to set rules and regulations. Eibl-Eibesfeld[10] has suggested that the sea-lizards or iguanas of the Galapagos Islands are a particularly good example of this behavior. Other species only begin to show signs of a special inhibition against killing or injuring members of the same species when they reach a certain age. The half-grown young of an African cichlid, *Lamprologus congolensis,* which are notoriously given to eating younger members of the same species, develop from the time that they become sexually mature an inhibition against this form of killing, despite their experience of it at an earlier stage.

This inhibition that prevents one member of a species from killing other members may depend not only on age and sex, but also on disposition. This is a well-known phenomenon which occurs especially in the form of a sudden, uninhibited attack on the part of an animal which feels itself cornered. The Chinese military expert, General Sun Tzu, who lived in the fourth century B.C., observed: "Do not press a cornered animal further back into the wall." Tu Yu, an early commentator, added: "As Prince Fu Ch'ai said, 'Wild animals fight with desperation when they are cornered and this is even more true of man. As soon as he realizes that he has no escape, he will fight to the death.' "

In this case, even the inhibition that is necessary for

83

self-preservation, preventing the animal or man from going too far, is abandoned. Being able to give up is as important to a living organism as the inhibition against killing a rival of the same species. Professor Tinbergen, the well-known Oxford ethologist, has often stressed the biological point-lessness of inhibiting this need to give up and of calling steadfastness to the point of death heroic.[64] One particularly striking aspect of this attitude is that men also regard it as heroism in animals when they do not give up. Just as fighting cocks and bulls are bred in certain parts of the world for the sole purpose of fighting, so too have the Siamese been breeding the fighting fish, *Betta splendens,* since 1850 and the little wrestling halfbeak, *Dermogenys pusillus,* since 1863. What is above all sought in the case of these little fish is that they refuse to give up the fight. Wild male fighting fish seldom fight for longer than fifteen to twenty minutes, but thoroughbred males will go on fighting for six to twenty-four hours. The basic methods of fighting have, however, not changed. Rivals which are as well matched as possible are set to fight each other, and the result is decided usually on points. "The aim," as I have said elsewhere in my book on the breeding of aquarium fish,[72] "is to push the limit at which one of the partners begins to retreat further and further back, so that the fish have enough time not simply to damage each others' fins, but to do something quite unbiological—to pull them out completely."

Wrestling halfbeak hardly ever injure each other when they fight, but it often happens that one of the combatants dies of utter exhaustion. We may therefore say that suicidal tendencies are present not only in the case of species with very dangerous weapons and that it is important to all rivals to be able to give up, whether or not they can injure their partners. This is why we find fights similar to single jousting combats between members of species such as the carp, which cannot harm each other because they have no weapons. Nothing ever happens during such fights and they can, of course, last for a very long time until one combatant defeats not his opponent, but himself, if he does not give up in time and seek flight. It is precisely for this reason that many formal elements of flight are found in combats between carp. The same also applies to the fights which take place between species with dangerous weapons, but which are not themselves dangerous because they are fought according to fixed rules and regulations. These duels last much longer than fights which are carried out with the purpose of injuring or damaging.

Instead of considering members of the same species in the abstract, it is possible to look at the various social partners whose lives may be threatened in different ways. The extreme danger, of course, is the danger of death by killing, but there are also preliminary stages, all of which are, if possible, avoided. Among the various forms of extreme danger are suicide; infanticide; killing the old; killing sexual partners; killing rivals; killing strangers.

a) Suicide
We shall not be able to know with any certainty whether animals are able to commit suicide so long as suicide is defined as a "conscious negation of one's own life" and we are unable to ascertain whether animals have a conscious mind of their own. However, we can say with absolute certainty that animals can endanger their own lives, and that one way in which they do this is by fighting with rivals. There are also many other modes of behavior which help to preserve the species as such and to increase the chances of survival of other members of the species, but which do not benefit the individual in this way. The prime goal for

the individual is not to survive itself, but to beget as many offspring as possible. In spite of its many disadvantages, the mule has as much power of resistance as its parents, the horse and the donkey, although it has no advantages as far as natural selection is concerned, because it is sterile. From this point of view, then, that of natural selection, the most suitable individuals are the father and mother of the biggest family. If a long period of parental care is required before the offspring is fully capable of reproduction, the number of children produced is less important in measuring the aptitude of the individual than the number of its grandchildren or later descendants.

The greatest advantage, of course, would result from action furthering the spread of the same genotype and avoiding everything that is in opposition to this. It may even be of great benefit to the preservation of the genotype, though not to the individual bearing this genotype, if the parent defends the young to the point of self-sacrifice. The success of this behavior can be seen clearly enough in the case of man when the individual behaving in this way goes as far as martyrdom. One spectacular act of self-sacrifice can often win a great number of followers for the movement as a whole. As Tertullian said, the blood of the martyrs is the seed of the Church.

Altruism regularly occurs in the animal kingdom when offspring need help. The interest of the community, the common good, takes precedence over self-interest and is in fact no more than genotypic interest. From this need to defend and preserve the young of the species has developed, for example, the typical warning cry against enemies, which warns many members of the group and endangers one member at the most. In the case of social insects, the caste of workers or soldiers has arisen as a result of this need. These specialized insects, themselves incapable of reproduction, are constructed simply and solely for the purpose of furthering the reproductive chances of a few members of the same species.

There is in man too a type of self-sacrifice which is close to suicide. This manifests itself noticeably in groups of people who are particularly exposed to natural selection by environmental factors. At the turn of the century, the Russian peasant would say: "*Tchujoi vek zayedayu, pora na pokoi*"—"I live other people's life: it is time to retire." And he did so.

Kropotkin writes: "The old man asks himself to die. He himself insists upon this last duty towards the community, and obtains the consent of the tribes; he digs out his grave; he invites his kinfolk to the last parting meal. His father has done so, it is now his turn; and he parts with his kinfolk with marks of affection."[28] But Kropotkin is also aware of the inhibition against killing. "But the savages, as a rule, are so reluctant to take anyone's life otherwise than in fight, that none of them will take upon himself to shed human blood, and they resort to all kinds of stratagems, which have been so falsely interpreted. In most cases, they abandon the old man alone in the wood, after having given him more than his share of the common food. Arctic expeditions have done the same when they no more could carry their invalid comrades . . . may be there will be some unexpected rescue!" The exposure of old and sick people and infanticide are part of a strict moral code.

Enough has been said and written about what happens in extreme cases for us to know the way in which old and sick people express their wish to die when they begin to feel that they are a burden on the community. We also know how this is received and carried out by others and the kind of inhibitions against killing and the conflicts of interest that emerge in such cases, because the community sees old

87

people, with their long experience, as a valuable possession. The wish to die has, generally speaking, begun with the old themselves. Freuchen[16] has observed that Eskimos long for their lives to end when they are very ill, when they are weighed down by serious anxieties and troubles and when, as they themselves say, "life is heavier than death." "In many places," Freuchen reports, "voluntary death is normal for old men and women who are burdened with the memories of their youth and can no longer meet the demands of their own reputation. Old people kill themselves to avoid being a hindrance to their kin." The way in which they die differs according to the tribe. What is more important, however, is why they choose to die. They do so because they are anxious about their relatives, "coupled with the sorrow of not being able to take part in the things which are worthwhile . . . In some tribes, an old man wants his oldest son or favorite daughter to be the one to put the string around his neck and hoist him to his death. This was always done at the height of a party where good things were being eaten, where everyone—including the one who was about to die—felt happy and gay."

Raymond de Coccola[7] has described the following scene. "I had been sampling the victuals in silence with the rest, studying the people after our protracted separation. I felt the gap left by the grandmother's death. 'When did Manerathiak die?' I asked Kakagun. 'Long ago during the summer. She was getting too old and useless.' 'What happened to her, Kakagun?' 'I don't know. We had pitched our tents at the mouth of the Siorkretak River. It was a rainy, windy morning. She walked along the shore to the cliffs overlooking the bay. She did not come back.' 'And you don't know where she went?' They all stared at me in astonishment. Nokadlak chuckled: 'She went to the top of the highest cliff facing the sea. The weather was stormy, the waves angry and high. She simply disappeared, Fala.' *'Mammianar!* Manerathiak knew the ways of your ancestors,' I said. 'She was a true Krangmalek woman.' After that epitaph no one mentioned her name any more."

Hermanns[21] has reported very similar cases in Asia. He mentions, for example, the Pantaram of South India, a nomadic tribe of poachers who bitterly struggle to survive, and the Siberian Yakut, who killed their old people when they were seventy, whether they wanted to die themselves or not. The one who was condemned to death was choked by raw meat or taken into the forest and either buried alive or left to die of starvation. Sometimes a father would ask his eldest son to pierce his heart, in the manner of the Chukchi, with a lance.

Even if we would not express it ourselves, hardly any one of us would object to this wish to die out of consideration for others. We know that animals that are old often voluntarily leave the society to which they belong without waiting to be ejected by the others of the group. So far, no one has done any extensive research into the reasons for this or into the changes in behavior that accompany it. I suspect, however, that anyone studying this matter in animals would find many indications as to the ways in which such behavior is conditioned in man.

b) Infanticide

It hardly needs to be said that a species or a population can ill afford to bring up too few young. If the number of individuals is to remain the same, each male and female parent must bring up two young in the course of their lives and these two will then replace their parents. If the parents produce fewer young, the species will die out, if they rear more than two, the species will increase. Since, however, most species produce more than two young per two parents, but the number of individuals still remains more or less constant—even in the case of fish such as the carp with the proverbial millions of eggs that the female lays—most of the offspring must clearly disappear.

Three obvious reasons for this disappearance are disease, enemies and accidents. Quite apart from these causes, however, young still disappear because there is not enough to eat. This does not mean that many die of starvation; on the contrary, they are killed by others of the same species. This is reasonable enough, because all are affected by the process of starvation—each one has something to eat, but none has enough to sustain life. In competing for food, the stronger and larger are in a privileged position. It also happens that offspring are directly killed (I shall return to this later). Once again, a delicate balance is preserved here, with the killing of offspring playing an essential part under certain conditions.

Man also commits infanticide, but again subject to certain conditions. By infanticide, I do not mean abortion, which also comes within the scope of the commandment "You shall not kill," but which is viewed more often intellectually than emotionally. Deformed infants were often killed until the nineteenth century in Silesia. Many of the female offspring of primitive peoples are killed as soon as they are born because they are less useful in hunting and require a dowry, which makes them a heavy burden on the family. This happens frequently among the Eskimos.[16]

In the case of the Bushmen, children are completely dependent on their mothers' milk for a very long time. This means that a mother who already has a child of about twelve months or less must, if she gives birth to another baby, either kill one of the children or else simply watch both children die.[38] Even the Germanic father had the right to expose one of his children or to have it exposed. This practice was forbidden in 1125 by Otto of Bamberg, who missionized the Pomeranians. The well-known fairy tales of Hansel and Gretel or Snow White are clear examples of this custom of exposing children.[2]

Older children were and are killed only in cases of extreme poverty. (Peter Freuchen has described this in very striking terms with regard to the Eskimos.)[16] Otherwise, the child's life is safeguarded as soon as a drop of food has passed its lips. There are two reasons for this. The first is that the child becomes fully human as soon as it has partaken of nourishment, whether from its mother or from a wet nurse, whether milk or, say, honey. The second reason is that the mother feels closely tied to the child as soon as she has nursed it.

This second reason, of course, has a biological basis. In the case of many mammals, the mother does not react fully as a parent to the young until she has suckled it. Various factors play a part here, according to the species—olfactory signs, for example, the mother's hormones and certain infantile signs in the young. This biological bond between mother and child develops very quickly and imposes severe limits on the possibilities of exchange and adoption.

The human infant is in many cases not regarded as a full human being by its own family or even by its mother for a short time after it has been born. There are biological reasons for this too, but although these can be used to explain why infants are often killed very soon after birth, they cannot provide justification for this practice. It is worth noting one aspect of this question briefly in passing. The synthetic family has been suggested as a sensible solution to the problem of countless orphans and unwanted children on the one hand and of the necessity to limit births on the other. Child adoption must be used to achieve this aim and the biological basis of adoption has in this case to be fully investigated, so that possible difficulties may be recognized and overcome.

Rituals of adoption, in which the offering of the breast plays a part, are also found among adults. Friendly Indonesians visiting a Papuan village have, for example, to suck briefly at the breast of the headman's wife.[11] Prince Kropotkin has said: "In the Caucasus, when a feud has been ended, the guilty party touches the breast of the oldest woman of the tribe with his lips and thus becomes a 'milk-brother' of all the men of the injured family." The adventures of a young man in a Turkish fairy story are relevant here. He successfully goes through these adventures because he has grasped the breasts of the female demon whom he has met and sucked them, so that she cannot harm him. I have dealt in some detail elsewhere with the extended function of the female breast in forming partnerships and as a social sign in animals and man.[71]

Very much more has still to be discovered about the biological basis of the relationships between mother and child on the one hand and between adults in partnership on the other, before the symptoms of faulty social behavior can be treated and their causes remedied. We are all aware of the mother's promptness to defend her child in danger. Yet, at the same time, it is an established fact that more children are killed every year in Germany by their parents than by strangers. Neither of these characteristics are purely human—they are shared by many animals.

c) The Killing of Rivals

I have already discussed one important aspect of this question in some detail: this is the case in which the commandment "You shall not kill" is illustrated by examples from the animal kingdom. In this instance, living organisms which are capable of inflicting severe injuries on the fighting partners or even killing them almost always possess certain mechanisms which prevent them from doing this in the interest of preserving the species.

In most cases of fighting between rivals, the object of the combat is food, a female, a special preserve or territory, which may have to be acquired in order to gain possession of food or a female, or shelter, either for the individual or for the offspring. Fights occur to keep the distance that individuals try to preserve between each other and, as it were, carry around with them wherever they go like a special territory. There are, however, other fights between rivals without any apparent objective at all, fights which very often result in the death of one of the combatants.

Young eagles provide a very good example of this kind of rivalry. Eagles usually lay two eggs, the second a few days after the first, and the young hatch one after the other accordingly. Leslie Brown,[6] one of the leading experts on eagles, has described the "Cain-and-Abel fight" that invariably breaks out between the two young eagles shortly after hatching. Either the older or the younger chick may begin the fight, but the winner is almost always the older, whether it is a male or a female. The attacker adopts the threatening attitude taken by adult eagles at the approach of enemies—the head extended, the wings half stretched, the bird itself sitting back on its tarsi. The two birds then begin to peck at each other, usually aiming at each other's back. One follows the other for hours round and round the nest, the stronger bird attacking the weaker partner, often tearing a wound already inflicted wider and wider. Both birds screech the whole time, but the parents never interfere, even if they are in the nest or near it. The fight may last for as long as two days, before the younger bird is dead.

Cranes and several other birds of prey also practice a similar form of fratricide or sororicide. The problem of the biological significance of this behavior has so far not been solved, but research into the behavior of related species in this respect has yielded some interesting data. In the case of the imperial and the lesser spotted eagles, for example, the younger chick almost always dies in combat with the older one. It survives, however, in one out of every five cases in the case of the golden eagle, the tawny eagle and Bonelli's eagle. Because the combat is less developed in the case of the white-tailed and the African sea eagles, the chance of survival is even greater.

There is no question in this instance of any inhibition against killing. These examples of very striking aggression between members of the same species have so far not been the subject of very extensive research, perhaps because birds of prey are automatically assumed to be aggressive.

The young eagle does not fight its brother or sister for food or for one of the recognized reasons mentioned above. They fight, strictly speaking, not as rivals, but simply as fighting partners. Adult eagles do not do this. They seldom fight each other at all, although they have very large preserves or territories.

d) The Killing of Males and Females

The number of possible offspring in a given population is determined by the number of female eggs produced by the female and ultimately, of course, by the number of females. The female of the species is consequently extremely important. We may therefore expect inhibitions against attacking females to be very effective. Taken as a whole among all the various social companions females are almost always the best protected against being killed by other members of the species. The fairly common case, among lower animals, of young eating their mother after they are born is a very special form of parental care of the young, in which the young make use of the mother, who is doomed to death, as food.

The male of many species of praying mantis and spiders is killed and partly or completely eaten by the female during or after mating. In such cases, selection is directed towards the offspring and the male takes care of the provision of offspring by the act of mating. Afterwards, there is no selective need to prevent the male from being killed. Another example of this killing of males is the well-known extermination of the superfluous drones in a community of bees. In considering the inhibition against killing in general, however, it is important to make a distinction between these cases.

e) The Killing of Strangers
George Schaller has made some interesting discoveries as a result of extensive field studies into the behavior of lions. In the first place, lionesses often simply abandon their young when there is too little food. (This is, of course, infanticide as the result of necessity by means of withdrawal of maternal care.) Secondly, however, in a few cases at least, male lions which have seized the harems of other, usually aged lions very often kill the young, dependent lions taken over with the harem. What they never do, however, is to attack their own young. It is not yet clear what selective effect this killing of young lions has.

The different colors used by beekeepers around the flight holes of their hives to facilitate the return of the bees to the right hives are, in fact, an adaptation to the absence of any inhibition on the part of bees against killing other bees from another hive. It is well known that each hive has a different smell, which makes it possible to recognize a stranger in the hive. In our context, however, what is important is that there is no sign of any inhibition preventing the killing of a member of the same species. But why do bees of one hive kill others from another hive which bring food into the hive?

There are, I believe, two possible reasons for this. Firstly, in the case of honeybees as in the case of other social insects, parasites may try to plunder their neighbors' supplies. Strangers may therefore mean danger, and attack at the very beginning is often the best defense. Secondly, the collector bees inform the others in their hive the direction in which they have found food and how far away from the hive this source of food is. They also recruit others to fly there. They do not, however, use the way back to the hive, but the way out from the hive to the source of food to indicate the destination. If they return, after flying out to collect food, to a different hive from the one they left, they give a wrong direction in this second hive. This wrong direction is, of course, the one which should have been followed from the first hive in order to reach the source of food. If the hives are at a greater distance from each other than is usual in an apiary, the directions given may be seriously wrong. Like the Australian aborigines, then, bees also seem to protect themselves against such "false doctrines."

The possible consequences of tolerating strangers in a hive have not yet been examined in detail. The worker bee is, of course, sterile, but in societies in which all the members were capable of reproduction it would clearly be an advantage to exclude or kill deserters, because they would have a harmful effect on their own society by withdrawing their labor and reproductive power. If their own society cannot win them back when they desert to another society, then again it is obviously to the advantage of loyalty to ones own society for each society to come, as it were, to a gentlemen's agreement and exclude or even kill the deserters who come to them from other societies, because

96

these intruders would only introduce an element of social disloyalty. Such speculation is really very helpful here. What does, on the other hand, emerge most strikingly from these findings is that the inhibition against killing does not apply simply to members of the same species. It is in fact limited at the most to fellow members of the same social group.

Later in this book I shall be dealing with the question of the selective advantage that results from traditions that are peculiar to the group. (The information exchanged between collector bees is something that is very close to this kind of tradition.) I shall at the same time show how these traditions help to eliminate competition. In view of this, it is not difficult to understand why many organisms enjoy peaceful relationships only with members of their own small group and keep strangers at a distance. In other words, such animals treat only fellow members of the same group in the way in which we might expect them to treat all other members of their own species.

This behavior is closely paralleled in that of man. Although he applies the commandment not to kill to his fellow man, he also frequently limits it to the fellow man who is simply a member of his own group. A good example of this limitation is to be found among the gypsies, who call themselves *rom* or "men," because, as the gypsy author Matéo Maximoff has said, "the gypsy is for us a man, but the others are not men. We call them by the name of *gadgés,* which means 'strangers.' "⁹

Similarly, many Papuan tribes on New Guinea refer to themselves as "We people," their word "man" meaning more or less the same as "tribal brother." Again, the first man is the tribal ancestor, not only for the Papuans, but also for the East African Kikuyu, whose "Adam" is simply known as "Kikuyu." "Bantu" too is simply "man," and the man who is not a Bantu still finds it difficult to obtain a post in the government of the east African states—especially if he belongs to the Masai, who also regard themselves as the real "people." It would not be difficult to continue with these examples *ad infinitum,* but one conclusion is obvious —if those outside the tribe or clan are strangers and not real people, then women can easily be classified as less than human when tribal exogamy is practiced.

It is clear from research into animal societies and into primitive tribal societies of men that differences in group traditions and norms develop. The way of life among neighboring groups of Australian aborigines,[12] of Papuans in New Guinea,[39] of Bushmen[58] and of South American Indians[3] can be quite different. Each group regards its own way of life as correct and that of its neighbors as wrong.

The group's assessment of the correctness and practical value of its own way of life, however, is almost always given an additional ethical flavor, so that this correct way of life is also seen as good and the way of life followed by others is not only wrong, but also evil. Thus, these "others" come to be regarded as evil strangers and are treated with hostile prejudice. At best, they are viewed with mistrust and are given the chance to prove that they are less evil than expected. This disdainful attitude is familiar to us—members of one profession or trade—in our treatment of those who have been differently educated or trained. In such cases, specialized "trade" jargon plays a prominent part in accentuating this contrast.

Recently, the moderate student leader Sam Brown criticized the American president Richard Nixon for calling students "bums," and asserted that Nixon was making it easier for a member of the National Guard to point his rifle at one of them and squeeze the trigger. The President had spoken of students in this way on May 1, 1970; on May 4, the National Guard shot four students on the campus of Kent State University—students who were proved to have been peaceful. "You have heard that it was said of the men of old, 'You shall not kill . . .' But I say to you that . . . whoever insults his brother shall be liable to the council, and whoever says, '*Raca*,' 'You fool!' shall be liable to the hell of fire" (Matt. 5. 21).

From the biological point of view, this New Testament statement is a very reasonable sharpening of the Fifth Commandment of the Old Covenant, and shows a deep insight into the structure of human behavior. Ovid's *Principiis obsta*—"prevent the first beginnings"—is a phrase that many of the older generation had to learn at school, but it is important to translate this dictum now, not so much into English, as was done in the past, as into the activity of everyday life.

Attempts are constantly being made to integrate unemployed people, foreign workers, minority groups and even simply "beginners" into the working communities of factories, banks and offices. Yet how often do these attempts fail because of the attitude of the other workers and even of those in charge or of those responsible for training. The social environment is frequently made uninviting and even destructive by their rough jokes. Initiation rites are usual in almost every group. They may be socially harmless like baptism, exuberant like the ceremony that takes place on crossing the Equator or reprehensible like attempted murder.

Digression:
Is Aggression a Spontaneous Need?

EVEN if all the distinctions outlined in the previous chapter are carefully observed, it is still possible to criticize the arguments put forward by ethologists to justify aggression. Whatever definition of aggression is accepted, there can be no doubt that it exists. What is really in question, however, is whether it is reactive or endogenously spontaneous, and above all whether it is cumulative. Is it an urge that must be discharged? If so, does the strength of this urge increase with the length of time since the previous discharging?

Originally, it was assumed that an organism possessed numerous reactions with which it responded to various situations in its environment. The organism's reactions were biologically meaningful, in other words, it recognized prey as prey and an enemy as an enemy and it knew it should seize and hold off the prey and avoid the enemy, because of what was known as instinct. When modern ethology was in its infancy, however, Lorenz emphasized that a structure of reactions of this kind was insufficient. For example, if a hungry fox simply sat until something that he could eat passed in front of his mouth, he would clearly die of hunger. Every creature that is not living in a fool's paradise has to go out in search of its food as soon as it experiences hunger. The hunger signal comes from within the body and, in reacting to it, the animal is not reacting to a stimulus from its environment. Nor does it simply react by *catching* prey, but by *looking* for prey. This search for prey, for example, when stimulated by appetite, is usually known as appetence behavior. It is this that leads the organism, which can make use of its experience in this process, to its prey or food and it is only when the food has been discovered that it is caught and devoured. As this appetence behavior increases, the demands that the organism makes with regard to the object that it has to look for often diminish. A thoroughly well fed dog cannot be enticed to leave his basket even if he is offered exceptionally tasty meat. Yet the same dog will accept very unattractive meat, old bones and even moldy bread, to which he would normally not react at all, if he has been looking for food for a long time. The reaction threshold is lowered, or, as a German proverb puts it, the devil will eat flies when he is pressed ("beggars can't be choosers").

A species may, for example, be on the verge of extinction if the adults avoid each other and individuals are at the same time dying because of enemies, accidents and disease. Individual members of the same species but of different sex have to seek each other out and produce more offspring, if only to correct the balance and make up for losses. The search for a sexual partner, then, is also appetence behavior.

It is not difficult to see that this type of behavior forms an essential part of those impulses which have to be used to make up for deficiencies either in food, in the case of the individual, or in individuals, in the case of the species. Does this apply to all instinctive and impulsive behavior? According to Lorenz,[36] a lowering of threshold and appentence behavior are as pronounced in a number of instinctive modes of behavior as they are in the case of aggression between members of the same species. Leyhausen[32] even claims that the same characteristics apply here as to fear or the impulse

101

to seek flight. In both cases, however, the consequences may be biologically absurd.

For example, an animal that has succeeded in expelling all disturbing competition from its own territory may after a while experience an appetite to fight and look around for others to disturb. To take another example, an animal inhabiting an island that is free from enemies may experience an appetite to run away and finally frees some biologically meaningless enemy substitute.

Too little research has up till now been done into the comparison of impulses for us to be able to provide a really satisfactory answer to these problems. Ethologists still do not know—and many of them seriously doubt—whether the working hypothesis that has hitherto been used, namely that all impulses have the same basic structure, can continue to produce the necessary results. The well-known scientific principle of economy, *principia interpretationis praeter necessitatem non sunt multiplicanda,* urges us not to apply new interpretations unless we are compelled to. It should not, however, make us blind to the possibility of new interpretations or difficulties with the older ones. We have ultimately to admit that we do not really know whether the aggressive urge and the urge to look for food are different, in what way they are different and how we ought to interpret it if they are not in fact different. But we do expect their physiology to reveal differences.

In view of what is known even at the present stage, it is not possible to agree with any general claim that aggression is an authentic instinct with its own endogenous stimuli and corresponding appetence behavior.

As early as the eighteenth century, Reimarus distinguished being able to act from the need to act: "How is it that, as soon as it has emerged from the egg, the spider makes the effort to weave such an artistic web from the superfluous juice that flows from its rear?" The question is whether aggression is an innate impulse which gives rise to an increasing need to fight in an organism that suffers from a biological deficiency because it does not have adequate opportunity to fight. It is, of course, possible to do research into this problem with animals that have grown up either under experimental conditions or in complete isolation, and to discover whether such organisms have an innate familiarity with their rivals or display modes of behavior in combat that are typical of the species (or demonstrate neither). This form of research, however, can never provide an answer to the question because it is directed towards two other adaptations, as discussed earlier in this book (p. 25).

The question is not whether the animal recognizes the situation that causes the stimulus or is able to fight in the way that others of the species fight, but whether it experiences an increasing urge to fight. In other words, does this urge increase of its own accord without having to be provoked externally by the animal's environment? It is, after all, well known that what the individual has experienced beforehand and the various conditions imposed from outside have a powerful influence on the animal's readiness to fight. Four groups of experiment can be conducted in connection with this question:

1. *Isolated Rearing.* It is possible to learn from the behavior of animals that have never been provoked by members of the same or of a different species whether experiences of this kind—provocation, frustrations and so on—are necessary for the accumulation of aggression. It is only when the aggressive behavior is either passive or else much stronger than usual (perhaps because it is directed towards an opponent) that this can be done. Additional tests have to be made to ascertain whether the same individual is in

general more excited or less excited than members of the same species which have grown up normally, and how its other impulses have developed. It is only in this way that we can learn whether the physiology of aggression can in fact exert an autonomous influence. None of the experiments conducted so far have produced clear-cut results.

2. *Temporary Isolation.* Adult animals—not half-grown ones—are usually isolated for a period of time from all contact with others of the same species. Here we are no more aware than we are in the following two types of experiment how a given aggression originally came about. We can, however, find out by testing whether this innate or acquired aggressive behavior shows spontaneous variations or whether the impulse is cumulative. This can be seen if the animal's aggressive behavior "idles," or if the animal reacts violently to test stimuli. Heiligenberg's experiments on an aggressive African cichlid (*Lamprologus congolensis*)[20] have certainly shown that aggressiveness atrophies in isolated animals. We are, however, not yet sure whether this atrophy is only a characteristic of aggression, or whether other impulses are also affected by it.

3. *The Training of an Isolated Animal with "Sight of a Rival" as a Reward.* In this case, the animal has to learn how to carry out some action (for example, how to successfully get through certain passageways in a maze) at the end of which it is rewarded by a glimpse of a rival. It is possible to conclude from the frequency with which the animal carries out the required appetence action the extent of the urge to fight which impels it to seek an opponent. Very diverse species can in fact learn in this type of test to carry out appetence actions, although it is seldom clearly a question of an appetence to fight. Such tests have never asso-

ciated another action with a different reward in order to determine what the animal might otherwise have been seeking.

Finally, the obvious assumption to be drawn here is that the animal will learn to regard the beginning of the maze, which is always visible, as a part of its rival or as the rival's disguise (*pars pro toto*). In this case, it is constantly exposed to whatever it associates with its rival, such as a (territory) marking; is consequently no longer isolated from that opponent; and therefore does not become spontaneously aggressive. It is well known that a dog will become as angry when it encounters the scent mark of a rival with which it has become familiar as with the rival itself.

(To the best of my knowledge, of all the experiments in which attempts have been made to persuade animals to perform certain actions by providing a situation calling for flight as a reward, none have succeeded. This certainly does not point to any need for flight or to any endogenous or spontaneous impulse to run away.)

4. *Temporary Isolation of a Pair.* Experiments with pairs of fish, chromide of the genus *Etroplus,* have shown that after a period of isolation the males attack their females and fight them, often eventually killing them, but that this does not happen if they are able to contact members of the same species. The obvious interpretation of this behavior is that the male's increasing desire to fight will, if no suitable object is available, eventually prove stronger than his inhibition against aggressive behavior towards his mate and he will get rid of the tension by attacking her.

These chromide, however, which keep the same sexual partner, are not sexually dimorphic. The male and female, in other words, look exactly the same. Very careful experiments carried out by Heiligenberg[20] have proved that this

105

fish's readiness to fight only increases when it sees a rival. If the female looks very similar to or exactly the same as the rival, this will inevitably increase the male's eagerness to fight. We may therefore conclude that the male that attacks his mate is not necessarily working off endogenous and spontaneous aggression. It may well be aggressiveness evoked by the female whose appearance is the same as the male rival. If this is so, the much quoted experiments in which pairs are isolated are clearly quite unsuitable tests of a spontaneous accumulation of aggression.

If the male and female of a pair incite each other to fight and if their partnership simultaneously acts as an inhibition against attack, the desirable biological result would be that they would both react with extreme aggression against any third which appeared as an enemy. It might also explain why animals that have mated so often defend their young so violently. Lorenz has discussed this question in his book on aggression,[36] where he takes as his example the mother turkey defending her young with such violence against all enemies on the ground, such as stoats, weasels and polecats, and, of course, rats.

The signal by which the mother turkey recognizes these hostile animals is "furry." Her own chicks, however, also send the same signal because they are downy. They therefore also arouse their mother's aggression, but at the same time inhibit any attack by their chirping. If they do not chirp or if the mother is deaf, the chicks are almost always attacked and killed by the mother. It is clear, then, that even when this aggression is directed against animals that are hostile to the species, the animal does not become aggressive spontaneously, but as the result of signals of an enemy's approach—in this case, "borrowed" signals.

Finally, it must be added that other species of cichlid which also keep the same mate remain at peace with their partners for a long time even if they are isolated from each other. This does not mean, however, that they lose their aggression. On the contrary, they attack enemies at once. We must therefore conclude—and this is something that is probably true in the light of other findings as well—that aggression originated to a great extent independently. In other words, it arose convergently, as a process of adaptation, like the wings of insects and birds (see p. 31f.). Even in the case of closely related species, the structure of this aggressive mechanism is also physiologically very diverse, just as the wings of insects and birds are both used for flying, but are very differently constructed.

If these facts are not taken into account when considering the question of aggression, then the discussion will not take place at the level of our present knowledge of the subject. We know, for example, as the result of research, that there are several different variable impulses, each independent of the other, in many different organisms. We also know that these impulses can be related to characteristic modes of behavior and measured with the help of these. Ethologists have developed methods which enable us to distinguish between what is innate and what is learned or acquired, not only in the organism's "knowledge" of situations, but also in its "ability" to make movements and its "relating" those movements to the given situations.

As early as 1935, Konrad Lorenz[34] drew attention to the "merging together of instinct and training." This is, of course, the combination of what is innate and what is acquired in more complex forms of action and the learning of finer characteristics for typical situations within a given framework of coarser knowledge.

All the same, the question of innate knowledge and ability is always applied to unbiological single units or elements of behavior. It is frequently asked whether aggressive

107

behavior or even aggression itself is innate, when what should really be done is to investigate precisely what is innate in this aggressive behavior. Other scientists go to the opposite extreme and break down all behavior as far as possible into the contractions of individual muscular fibers and examine each of these in detail. The latter would clearly be better advised to select natural units of behavior appropriate to the level of the question itself. These would, of course, be those behavioral elements which would appear either alone or else in various combinations. The question hardly applies to smaller units of behavior and no unequivocal answer can be given to it in the case of larger elements.

All this has to be taken into consideration in deciding whether there is an innate, spontaneous and cumulative aggressive urge, and in what organisms it can be found if it does exist. "Innateness" can only be tested, as Lorenz stressed so often, by eliminating all other possible characteristics that have been acquired by learning and experience. "Spontaneity" in this case means a repeated change in the state of the individual, not a change in the state of its environment. The cumulative effect of aggression can be measured in four ways. Firstly, the intensity of the actions which characterize the impulse or urge in question can be measured. Secondly, the appetence behavior (the need to search) which is peculiar to the species or to which it has been trained can provide an accurate idea of the accumulation of aggression. In the third place, it is possible to measure how much the threshold is lowered for stimuli that release aggression, that is to say, with what substitute objects the organism is satisfied in order to work off its aggressive urge, including the actions performed when the aggressive urge is passive or "idling" and which therefore has no replacement object. Finally, we can measure the intensity

108

of accumulative aggression by using trained or specific inhibitions which prevent the organism from performing these actions. These may take the form of inhibitions against attacking mate or young, or tripwires or other obstacles on the way to the object.

It is seldom sufficient to apply only one of these four ways of measuring aggression. It is only possible to test whether the aggressive urge is cumulative by measuring the organism's readiness to perform nonaggressive actions as well, in which case it remains an open question whether an accumulation of aggression cannot be broken down in any other way apart from by characteristically aggressive behavior. It is well known that aggression induced from without can accumulate, and that a proved ability to store aggression does not necessarily also imply spontaneity.

Those who defend the thesis that aggression is spontaneous and cumulative are in danger of collecting data and findings that support this argument, as Leyhausen[32] did in the case of anxiety. If this thesis is to be critically tested, we have to find out whether the question of a spontaneous and cumulative impulse can be bypassed when all the data available have been carefully considered. If this is done, it will at once be apparent how much still remains unexplained.

There can be no doubt that all these factors can and must be investigated if the question heading this digression—is aggression a spontaneous need?—is to be properly answered. Yet no research has thus far been conducted into any living organism. What is more, we still lack the necessary comparisons from which we might be able to infer the phylogenesis and the adaptability of a supposedly aggressive urge. The well-known biological phenomenon of "spacing out," according to which a given species is distributed over as much as possible of the whole environment

109

that is suitable to it, need not be brought about by attacks on members of the same species. It can also be achieved by avoiding others, or their droppings or marks of their scent. Birds, for example, keep rivals at a distance by singing, but bird song is not regarded as typically aggressive behavior. The fact that the aggressive urge is useful for the purpose of spacing out does not necessarily mean that spacing out makes aggressive behavior essential.

The psychological and sociological data relating to human aggression can be compared experimentally with the data derived from ethological research into animals, but no theory of human aggression can be built up on the basis of research into animal behavior.

This will perhaps help to explain why, in almost all theories about aggression, the examples given from the animal kingdom seem to be no more than parables without any real value as comparisons. We may conclude by observing, in passing, that we are only now beginning to find answers to the same and similar questions in connection with impulses other than aggression.

Intercommunication
—You Shall Not Lie

"A LIE is a consciously false statement made to lead the partner in dialogue astray. It therefore either presents a datum or a situation of the inner reality or the outside world incorrectly or else changes it by surprising or distorting certain elements. Animals cannot lie, because they have no language." Kainz[26] wrote this in his book on the "language" of animals. To be sure, it is possible not only to *tell* a lie, but also to produce one by means of a deceptive mode of behavior. "But animals are not even capable of false presentations," Kainz continues, "because they cannot represent data or situations in naming symbols that are expressed in different forms and accompanied by clear, objective intentions. They cannot therefore represent these situations falsely."

Animals are, of course, capable of instinctive shamming and of pseudo-cunning deception. Examples of this kind of behavior are pretended death at the approach of an enemy and the habit of certain birds of drawing an enemy away from the nest by feigning to have a broken wing and hopping conspicuously away.

In such cases, however, the animal is acting without insight, just as a spider makes a meaningful and very complicated web to catch its food, doing this without insight and quite instinctively. Shamming in the real sense of the word, Kainz insists, is based on reflection, and animals are incap-

111

able of this. Borderline cases mentioned by Kainz include, for example, certain apes which outwit their keeper by stealing things from him and behaving innocently so that he does not notice. Other apes fill their mouths with water, entice people to come close to them, by begging or by feigning indifference, then spit the water at them. Kainz says that one might speak of lying behavior in such cases, but adds that examples of this kind have never been found in the natural state, but only among wild animals in captivity and in domestic animals. After all, he continues, only domesticated animals are able to build on to innate behavioral elements, use a certain insight to incorporate their own experiences into various modes of behavior and thereby have at their disposal possible deceptive maneuvers which are basically far more than purely instinctive actions.

Many conversations have convinced me that this is a very widespread view. What strikes me as particularly interesting, however, is that animals are believed to acquire insight and therefore the first condition for lying as soon as they are influenced by man. Lying is clearly regarded as man's unhappy privilege. I should like to show why this is, in my opinion, a false view. This may offer comfort to some people, albeit a cold comfort.

It is very interesting to compare a number of statements published in scientific and other more popular journals with affirmations made by scholars specializing in humane studies. Kainz has declared, for example, that all sounds forced from an animal must be produced in a form which is fully in accordance with the species itself. This means that no animal is, in his opinion, capable of uttering a cry of terror that is peculiar to its species in a situation that does not arouse fear. It cannot, in other words, simulate terror. I do not know how Kainz came by this information, but it is not difficult to refute his claim.

112

For many years, Doctor Gerhard Thielcke[62] and his wife Helga reared blackbirds and song thrushes in their laboratory in the Zoological Institute at Freiburg. The birds were safe from enemies and familiar with man. Cared for by experts, their development was quite normal. All the same, they developed a remarkable behavioral characteristic which has never been observed in blackbirds and song thrushes living in the wild state. Both species have a warning cry which they utter whenever anything threatening flies past. If a blackbird or a song thrush hears this call—a long drawn out *tseee*—it will at once seek cover or, if this is not to be found, remain motionless. The bird reacts, in other words, without first ascertaining for itself whether there really is danger or not. The birds brought up indoors at Freiburg at first uttered this warning cry in the "right" situation, that is, for example, whenever a bird flew past the window outside the room. After a while, however, they also began to give "warnings" whenever another blackbird or thrush snatched a tasty morsel from their noses. Eventually, one or other of the birds would even sound the alarm as soon as the mealworms were brought to them, the one uttering the warning cry showing no sign at all of fear, the others, however, quickly seeking cover or remaining quite still for a little while, thus giving the one that had given the warning time to enjoy his meal undisturbed.

This clearly contradicts Kainz's statement. It is undeniably an example of the application of a specific warning cry to a situation in which the threat of danger was absent, accompanied by the very deception of members of the same species of which Kainz claims no animal is capable. Although it is fairly certain that this transference of the warning to a new situation contains many acquired elements, it is also true to say that the bird giving the warning did not have such a deep insight into the new situation that

113

it was completely immune to the warning cry itself. This is quite clear from the sequel to this pattern of behavior. Whenever the other birds rushed for cover and uttered the warning themselves, the thrush that had first sounded the alarm also reacted in the expected way and ran for cover too.

It is, of course, possible to object on the grounds that these are creatures living in close contact with man and therefore more prone to lie, although no one knows for certain how that works. It cannot be denied that the behavior described by the Thielckes has so far only been observed among birds in captivity. Yet we have only to pause for a moment and think about how much knowledge is required of the situation on the part of the observer before he can discover anything of this kind, and we will know at once how unlikely it is for such behavior ever to be scientifically observed in the wild state, even if it were to occur there.

We do, however, have information about the same kind of behavior in another animal living in the wild state. Dr. G. Rüppell[55] spent the summer of 1967 in a tent on the Diabasodden, a cliff in the Isfjord of West Spitzbergen, observing a pair of polar foxes and their four young. The vixen was in the habit of looking for food in the vicinity of Rüppell's tent and taking it back to her den about a quarter of a mile away. The hungry cubs would jump up at her and take the food away from her. On one occasion, the vixen had stolen a big piece of cheese and, when she came back with it, one of the cubs leaped at her, barking, and she dropped it. The cub stood beside the cheese, turned its hind quarters toward its mother, lifted its tail and urinated in her direction. Then it began to eat. The vixen moved around and watched, then suddenly raised her muzzle and gave the high-pitched warning cry several times. The cub dropped the piece of cheese at once and ran off quickly into the rocks. The vixen ran to the cheese and devoured it.

Although there was no recognizable danger in the vicinity, the vixen habitually drove her cubs away with the warning cry in most cases when she wanted food herself. She could not, of course, bite her young in order to send them away, because, as a mother, she had a pronounced inhibition against biting them. Polar foxes have no enemies on Spitzbergen and man is a very rare visitor. When he does appear, the foxes are so tame that they will eat out of his hand. It is quite clear, then, that this is a case of the enemy warning cry being used in a harmless situation with the purpose of deceiving members of the same species. This time, however, it occurs in the case of an animal living in the wild state and not in the case of one reared by human beings.

Rüppell reports that "deliberate lying" of this kind did not occur in comparable situations in the case of a second family of polar foxes living in a different place, so that the conclusion must be that this behavior is neither instinctive nor innate. It is not known how the vixen of the first family came to practice this trick. She may by chance have gained certain advantages from the effects of having used this warning cry previously in some other situation and, having learned from this experience, have begun to misuse the call. It is also conceivable that she foresaw that the cubs would run away on hearing her warning. This, of course, calls for a certain degree of insight and anticipation, or the first warning given in a situation of this kind would otherwise have been a lie. Certainly it was a lie on the subsequent occasions, no matter how the vixen came to use it in the first place.

There can, in any case, be no doubt at all that both the thrushes and the vixen were deliberately misusing an acoustic signal that was customarily employed as a means of communication between members of the species, and thereby gained an individual advantage at the expense of the others. The claim made by Kainz and others[52] that only man is capable of lying, and that lying is out of the question for animals because they have no language, is therefore obviously based on a wrong conclusion.

It is hardly necessary to point out that misuse of a warning cry by an individual for his own advantage cannot possibly become the universally valid norm in a society. As long as every member of the species reacts to it promptly, rivals will misuse it to intimidate each other in order to deprive each other of the reward both seek, so that it ultimately becomes meaningless. So long as the warning cry continues to be misused only by individuals, the others gradually come to mistrust them. Rüppell, in fact, observed this in the behavior of the polar foxes of Spitzbergen. He reports that although one cub continued after a while to move away from its mother when she gave the warning, it nonetheless crept back again with its tail between its legs. The mother repeated the warning several times, but without success. It is obvious that the cub had in the meantime learned that there was no danger despite the mother's warning cry. The consequence is equally obvious—the warning loses its value and no longer functions even when danger really threatens. You can, in other words, cry "wolf" once too often.

This is precisely why lying is universally forbidden in human society. It is not so much because something that is wrong is represented as right in a lie. The person who always says "black" instead of "white," "left" instead of "right," "hungry" instead of "satisfied" or "happy" instead of "sad" is not such a bad partner in conversation, because his idiosyncrasy can be taken into account and what he says can be understood in the right sense. It is the person who talks unpredictably first in one way and then in another who makes communication impossible and thus "lies." An organism that is dependent on social intercommunication cannot allow itself to indulge in lying.

Whenever collaboration and cohesion within the group are as vitally necessary as they are, for example, in the case of the Bushmen of the Kalahari, we find excommunication regularly pronounced as a punishment on any member who is proved guilty of a failure with regard to the group.[58] What is more, this is a sentence of excommunication in the strictest sense of the word. It is a breaking off of all communication with that person. Everything said by individuals who do not fit easily into the group because of temperamental or other difficulties is also politely but deliberately misunderstood. This makes their exclusion from the group more gradual and less painful.

The commandment "you shall not lie" is usually explained in this way today. In the legal language of the Old Testament, however, it is expressed as "you shall not bear false (or lying) witness against your neighbor." The Old Testament law was not concerned with lying in general, but with lying witness before a court, which itself merited death, and because of which an innocent man might be punished by death. This is explicitly stated in the deuteronomic law (Deut. 19. 18–20). "If the witness is a false (lying) witness and has accused his brother falsely, then you shall do to him as he had meant to do to his brother; so you shall purge the evil from the midst of you."

I admit that this version of the commandment seems to have been specially written for a typically human action and that it is hardly possible to assume that this type of behavior has its biological origins in the animal kingdom. Nonetheless it does, and we may say with certainty that this forbidden mode of behavior is not restricted to man.

Dr. Hans Kummer of the University of Zurich has been

117

observing hamadryas or sacred baboons (*Papio hama-dryas*) for many years both in captivity and in the wild state in Ethiopia. These baboons insist on a fairly strict observance of hierarchical values among the members of each troop. Whenever animals with a low rank go too far away from the troop or are too forward in seizing food, thus claiming a higher rank than they in fact possess, they are at once attacked by a baboon of higher rank. Their response to attacks of this kind is to make a gesture of submission. They turn their bright red buttocks towards the attacking baboon, thus pacifying him after an action during which he was particularly angry. They also do the same with the intention of preventing attack, for example, whenever they, as baboons of lower rank, pass another of higher rank so closely that the latter might interpret it as provocation. This kind of anticipatory gesture of pacification is clearly a kind of greeting.

Baboons can misuse this greeting and in fact do so most conspicuously in a situation in which three apes take part, one of the higher rank and two lower in the hierarchy, possibly equal to each other in rank. If, for any reason, one of these two threatens the other by screaming, by threatening mimicry or by combative movements, it often does so with its hindquarters turned towards the third ape, the one with a higher rank. The latter will almost always intervene in any quarrel and decide the matter by attacking one or other of the subordinate members of the community. If, however, the baboon that is disturbing the peace places itself with its buttocks facing the ape of superior rank, in the "greeting" attitude, the latter cannot attack it and has therefore to attack the ape that is threatened if he wants to make peace. The mischief-maker thus forces the senior ape, by his gesture of submission, to become angry with a third member of the group, although this third ape has given no

118

cause for anger. In this way, it is possible for an animal of low rank to have another of higher rank attacked and driven away by the baboon that occupies the highest rank.

The same type of behavior has also been observed in other species of baboon and in rhesus monkeys.[30] It seems to have been "invented" by different individuals who can thereby have innocent members of the species punished by the authorities. They are, in this way, undeniably acting as false witnesses. What is more, it is obviously a step towards placing self-interest above the common good.

In view of the fact we have demonstrated here—that lying or bearing false witness also occurs in the animal kingdom—it would be interesting to know how it is countered or overcome. Unfortunately, we have no information about this. All the same, we may be sure that there must be a countermechanism, because this behavior never in fact runs riot in the animal world. All that we can say with certainty is that the Eighth Commandment has a biological origin and that it is only sensible to investigate it.

Property
—You Shall Not Steal

"SHOW me a liar and I will show you a thief." In the Decalogue, stealing is forbidden twice, in the Seventh Commandment and in the Tenth. The Seventh Commandment originally applied to cases in which a free Israelite was stolen so that he could later be sold as a slave. "If a man is found stealing one of his brethren, the people of Israel, and if he treats him as a slave or sells him, then that thief shall die" (Deut. 24. 7). The Tenth Commandment deals with the criminal appropriation of other men's property.

It is hardly possible to deny that animals also have a tendency to take each others' property, an obvious example of this is fighting between members of the same species for preserves. Fritz Frank[15] has dealt in considerable detail with territory as personal property and with the territorial instinct as the origin of man's struggle to possess land and other things that are important to life. He emphasizes that "man's struggle to obtain personal property has long been regarded by those who oppose human nature and elevate his spirit as an invention of sinful or capitalist man. It is, on the contrary, an integral part of highly organized life and is as such several hundred million years old."

He may, of course, be right, but I believe that this is not the aspect of property that really interests us. He is concerned with property which is *contested,* which is coveted by others and is defended by its owner and continues to be

120

his property for as long as he manages to keep his competitors away from it. He will in fact succeed in doing this for as long as his courage, determination and ability to fight last.

The emphasis here, then, is on defense, on the *ownership* of property. But not every owner fights continuously for his own property. When once he has shown himself to be the stronger in any contest, his property will be respected for a while by others. He will, however, lose it as soon as he is no longer able to prove his worth. If, on the other hand, my assumption is correct, namely that the Ten Commandments are demands which did not first become necessary only when man began to evolve, then there must be mechanisms in the animal kingdom as well, other than the law of the strongest, which act as a check on the struggle for property. In this case, what we have to ask is not how much property an individual can defend, but rather how much the others will allow him to possess before he has to fight for it. The prior condition here, of course, is that property is involved at all, in other words, whether what all creatures are struggling to gain is property.

The hamadryas baboons mentioned in the previous chapter live in harem groups, that is, the adult males possess several wives. Hans Kummer has made several interesting discoveries as the result of exhaustive observations in the wild state and suitable experiments. (His work has recently been made into a film.) One of his findings throws light on the baboons' attitude towards property. As soon as a male and female have paired with each other, no other male tries to win that female. The only exceptions occur when baboons from different troops are mixed together with a resulting loss of control. Even in the case of two males in the same cage, one stronger than the other—to whom a female has already been given before the stronger baboon

121

was introduced into the cage—the stronger will not attempt to win the female. He will usually sit apart from the pair in a corner of the cage as though trying to disturb them as little as possible. If, on the other hand, he is given the female first, he will accept her without further ado, in which case the weaker male will behave in a disinterested fashion. The female is regarded by both as worth winning, but as soon as she has become the property of one of the apes, she is at once tabu for the other, even if he is the stronger of the two males. He will not show any sign of desiring the female and will do none of the tricks that he might otherwise do to gain possession of her.

I have already drawn attention to the fact that, in Israel, the neighbor's wife originally formed part of his property and was only later protected by the Ninth Commandment. The prehuman biological situation is clearly illustrated in the behavior of hamadryas baboons.

The young of all baboons and of many other apes and monkeys are particularly coveted by older members of the species. Childless females especially show a great desire to carry and nurse little ones and in many cases they perform the function of "aunts."[54] Young orphan hamadryas baboons are cared for by adolescent males who have just reached sexual maturity and the young generally are free to behave as foolishly as they like. Young langurs and hulmans, long-tailed Asiatic monkeys, are cared for in turn by all the females of the group and, if possible, suckled by them.[25] However coveted a young ape or monkey may be, however, its mother can always get it back. Even stronger females do not try to keep the young of another member of the species, which is always recognized as her property.

In the wild state, chimpanzees like to eat flesh. Dr. Jane van Lawick has frequently observed that they go hunting and catch small baboons and other apes and monkeys, wild

122

boar and even antelopes. The successful hunter then possesses flesh which is coveted by all the other chimpanzees. According to Dr. van Lawick, there is no doubt at all within the group as to who is the owner of the game. Even much more powerful males, who could without any difficulty take the game from the ape that had caught it, simply sit down beside him and ask him for a piece of meat by stretching out their open hands towards him. They are usually given something, but by no means always and frequently only after they have waited for a long time.[31] The important behavioral aspect here is not so much that the meat is distributed by means of asking and giving, but that the object that is coveted by the whole group is the property of one individual and consequently tabu for the others, who openly acknowledge the ownership of that individual.

Of the many other examples of this kind, let me give one, that of the Australian zebra finch. When they are looking for a place to nest, these birds often take over empty nests and use them to sleep in. They never enter a nest containing eggs or chicks. Even when the owner is away, this kind of nest is recognized by the zebra finch as privately owned and therefore as protected. In captivity, however, tame zebra finches often cease to observe this tabu.[24]

We may therefore conclude that it is undoubtedly possible for animals to lie and to steal and, what is more, that they also have at their disposal behavioral mechanisms which restrict or prevent this tendency to lie or to steal. The corresponding commandments of the Decalogue have the same task in the human sphere—that of solving a biological problem.

Sexual Partnership
—You Shall Not Commit Adultery

1

IN 1954, the Supreme Criminal Court of the Federal Republic of Germany declared that there is an objective moral law which is binding on all men and which is based on an existing scale of values to be accepted by all men. This moral law "places monogamy and the family before man as an obligatory way of life and makes them the foundation of life for all nations and states."

As we have already seen, quite early experiments on a few selected species revealed that environmental or ecological factors have a decisive influence on the structure of society and on that of the family. Assuming that the different social forms which are taken by the same or similar species are all adaptations to the environment which make survival under various circumstances easier for the species in question, we may also assume that the same applies to man. This question has been subjected to extensive research, which I cannot discuss here. It has, however, been known for some time that polyandry, which occurs in relatively few human societies, is almost always connected with certain forms of economy. In Tibet, for example, it hardly ever occurs among cattle-breeding nomads, but is found more frequently in the poorer agrarian regions. The reason is always the same—either a shortage of land or a shortage of water. As Hermanns has pointed out, "this odious practice has come about because of the infertility of the soil and the narrow strips of land which can still be cultivated despite the serious shortage of water. The harvest is sufficient only when all the brothers in a family continue to live together. If they were to separate and have families of their own, they would soon become beggars."[21]

The well-known Danish explorer, Peter Freuchen,[16] has said that polyandry is quite common among Eskimos because of a general scarcity of women, several men possessing one wife, and that hunters on very long journeys also have a right to intercourse with a woman other than their own wife. Sexual life and family life among Eskimos and other primitive peoples is never unregulated, however. Social relationships change, but not arbitrarily. They differ according to the prevailing circumstances. Gabus has drawn attention to the "principle of selection which applies not only to the cattle breeding activities of the Bororo, but also to the procreation of their own race. The inbreeding which they practice enables them to keep their blood pure. Their cult of beauty and the great importance they attach to physical perfection has led to the custom known as 'teggal.' This makes it possible for a young woman to leave her bridegroom or husband for a period varying between several months and two years and to live with the man whom she has chosen at the dance. Especially handsome young people are paired off as 'togo' or 'bearers of beauty' at tribal meetings. Husbands submit to this custom for racial reasons without the slightest feeling of shame or jealousy."[17]

It is therefore extremely important to examine the various forms of marriage and family life practiced among different peoples and those current within the same group at different times in history within the context of the factors conditioning life in the group or groups. This is because it is only

125

possible to apply a form of marriage or family life which is binding on all men to those groups among whom this appears to be lacking when we know exactly what other circumstances have to be changed to make it easy or even to make it possible for them to accept such a form of marriage and family life. As soon as we try to find out the factors that play a part in this process, of course, we realize at once how little we really know about it.

We should not, of course, apply this principle exclusively to people of different races or periods. We must also use it to find out whether different conditions exist or have existed simultaneously within a people, a nation or an ethnic group—above all, conditions that favor different forms of marriage in subgroups or at different levels. The same also applies to individuals who are subject to changing conditions throughout their lives. The individual clearly cannot change the form of his marriage according to the circumstances of his life, but it would be valuable to know whether it is possible to find at least some reasons for social tension —either within the family unit or in other relationships between individuals—in a more or less satsfactory adaptation between the social structure and the demands made by the environment.

Monogamy in human society is usually regarded as a higher stage of development. This evolution to the higher level of monogamy is, however, not found in the animal kingdom, in which none of the many different forms of marriage or family life, including monogamy, which is quite widespread among animals, appears regularly as the beginning or the end of a process of development. As far as we are able to reconstruct the evolutionary process, there is, in the animal kingdom, both development towards monogamy and development away from it. The same seems also to be true of the various forms of family life.

When the number of offspring is taken into consideration,

it is possible to measure with a fair degree of accuracy which form of marriage offers more advantages to the species under given conditions—seasonal or permanent mating, or a changing or life-long partnership. J. Coulson has investigated precisely this phenomenon over a period of twelve years' observation of a colony of kittiwake gulls.[8] Pairs of gulls that have bred successfully and stay together lay more eggs the following year, more eggs from which a higher percentage of hatched chicks become fully fledged young than in the case of birds of the same age that have changed their partners. For whatever reason, a change of sexual partner has a harmful effect on procreation and this effect can be discerned at least two broods later. The opposite effect of advantage to procreation can also be observed when the partners remain together.

Many gulls, however, change their sexual partner, not just because it has died or simply disappeared, but often as a consequence of a failed brood. This does not mean that the birds decided to separate because of their failure to raise young. On the contrary, it is far more likely that the failed brood and the separation of the two partners have the same cause, namely, that the partners were not suited to each other. If they separate, there is always a chance that a suitable partner will be found, in which case the brood will be less succesful than that of a pair which has been together for a longer period, but noticeably more successful than that of a pair of incompatible gulls. Coulson's findings, then, are clearly a very good example of the biological basis for a particular form of marriage.

As I have dealt in some detail with the "natural laws of marriage" in another book of that title,[71] I can confine myself here to two aspects of the subject which seem to me to be essential, firstly the phenomenon of lasting partnership and secondly sexual norms and the abuse of sex.

There are three factors which have to be taken into consideration in the case of a lasting partnership between two individuals. The first is that it may be a reciprocal bond which unites them. The second is a one-sided bond and the third is a bond tying both to some other object. It is often extremely difficult to discover what really binds animals or humans together in a lasting sexual partnership. We know with a fair degree of certainty that the stork, for example, practices place monogamy, that is, both partners are, to a great extent independently of each other, "married" to the same nest and come back year after year to that nest, where they meet again and bring up a family together. An anonymous form of marriage is also practiced by certain animals, each individual fighting all members of the same sex as rivals. The female drives all other females away and the male all other males, with the result that exactly two members of the same species but of different sex are able to live together. One partner can, however, be exchanged for another and, if a newcomer wins in combat with one of the partners, it replaces the vanquished partner.

Cases in which each individual knows its own partner and does not confuse it with other members of the species are, of course, of greater interest to us. Once again, however, it is very difficult to prove beyond doubt the occurrence of this individual recognition and to establish the cause of it. Clearly, it presupposes the existence of individual characteristics by which an individual can be distinguished from others of the same species and can also be recognized at once. For example, the larger of two members of the species cannot be recognized by its size if it appears alone or with another of exactly the same size. Yet, although the partner cannot be recognized by such relative characteristics and the marks which distinguish one individual from another are not characterized as such, it is only possible to separate them out by comparing them with other individu-

128

als. When individual members of a species recognize each other in this way, we can evaluate all the characteristics which are accessible to us and which contain the distinctive quality of the individual, but this does not mean that they can be named. It is essential to separate the individual characteristics out from the combined group of features if we are to prove scientifically how individuals can recognize each other.

In the case of many mammals, individual smell seems to be an essential characteristic of recognition, but it has not been possible to carry out many tests so far, as scents cannot be registered like sounds, colors or movements on a tape recorder or on film. Optical and above all acoustic signals are, however, much more accessible. It is still difficult to discover which are the really decisive characteristics when one member of a species recognizes another individual by its appearance, its way of moving or its visible behavior. On the other hand, it is relatively easy to find out the relevant sound characteristics when an individual is recognized by its voice, because only a few parameters (intensity, frequency and overtones) can play a part. For this reason, our knowledge of individual recognition among animals is greatest in the sphere of sound—recognition, in other words, by acoustic characteristics.

One of the most striking examples of this type of individual recognition is the acoustic ritual or duet performed by monogamous songbirds (and other birds) and by gibbons among the anthropoid apes. These duets take the form of antiphonal calls or melodies which are precisely in tune with each other and often recognizably individual in character. In some species, they are very simple, in others highly complicated. In almost all species, however, the ritual consists of fragments of precisely timed song exactly in tune with and corresponding to the partner's song. Partners can

129

clearly recognize each other by these acoustic signals, and by the theme that is characteristic of the pair. The very accurate timing and precise tuning in to each other, however, seems to have something to do with the bond that links the two individuals together.

Research workers in this field have often spoken about this "bond" between two individuals, and about the modes of behavior that accompany that bond and strengthen it. The scientist has to try to describe this bond in such a way that it can be understood as a scientific phenomenon. He also has to measure it so that there can be a measure of agreement about the way in which this bond is strengthened and so that he can compare what different writers have in fact said about it. A special research program is going on at present, with the aim of establishing the extent to which a behavioral state of being in tune with each other in the widest sense (acoustic rituals or duets are only one example of this behavior) can produce this effect of a mutual bond.

When two partners are accurately in tune with each other, the one will usually do precisely what the other "expects." There is a great deal of evidence to indicate that the central nervous system often works toward a certain state in which what takes place deviates as little as possible from what is expected, as though it were essential to keep a certain inner state as constant as possible. Captive animals have often been observed to make stereotyped movements, sequences carried out in precisely the same places and in exactly the same form.

Captive squirrels, for example, work off their need to move about, not by trying out new routes, but simply by repeating the same runs and jumps in the same places, where they can be quite certain of what will happen in their environment. They need to know exactly the direction in which each branch will bend and which board will creak

130

when they jump forward or roll backwards, going through every familiar movement as if they were "asleep." Free-living animals also behave in this way. Bats, for example, return from their nocturnal hunting expeditions by exactly the same way, following exactly the same pattern of flight each time. If a board is placed in front of their normal flight path into the cave where they sleep, they will invariably fly into it, not because they are not able to perceive it, but because they are behaving "as if they were asleep," relying on the expected and discounting what is unexpected.

Just as they prefer to follow familiar paths and carry out well-known movements in places where everything happens as they expect it to happen, so too animals prefer familiarity to unfamiliarity in their sexual partners. An animal will choose a partner who will correspond as closely as possible to its expectations. If it has to adapt its expectation to the reality of the situation, it becomes bound to the partner to which it has adapted itself. This is very similar to the observed behavior of squirrels, which show that they are, for example, very closely bound to one particular corner of the cage or enclosure to which they have adjusted or tuned their movements. It is possible that, by means of a kind of "economy switch" in the nervous system, which may be connected with the constant mechanisms, a mutual tuning in to each other produces a bond between the partners. (This has a psychological parallel in human society: a person finds it easy to relax among those whom he knows, but has to exert himself among strangers.)

Normally, it is impossible for any living organism to avoid all contact with strangers or unfamiliar environments. Consequently, every animal is obliged to adjust itself again and again to its environment and even to tune in repeatedly to the partner it already knows very well. In this way, sexual partners come to know each other better and better.

It can be no surprise to the ethologist that the biblical term for the most intimate marital relationship between partners is "knowledge." Genesis tells us not that Adam "begot" a son, but that "Adam knew Eve his wife" (Gen. 4.1). We may be certain that the human partner in marriage has a right to be known as an individual and not simply to be treated as property. The man who brands his fellow human being or marks him in any way as his property is not treating him or her as a human partner. On the other hand, however, it is often very important to know the characteristics which typify an individual's personality. In that case, it is a great advantage if that individual can be observed against as many different backgrounds and compared with as many other individuals as possible. Enclosing or isolating a fellow man or woman or keeping that person exclusively for oneself and away from others means that he or she will never be fully known in the biblical sense or recognized or known again in the biological sense as a partner. In the animal kingdom, some of the most striking bonds between individuals have been observed in wandering troops or pairs, species which are especially faithful to one territory or place tending to rely on a common meeting ground that is very familiar.

Seen in this light, partners in a marital relationship that is taken seriously have to remain together voluntarily. The first step towards separation is made when one partner says "no" to the other.

2

Like the other commandments, the commandment "You shall not commit adultery" referred originally to offenses which, like the legal provisions of other ancient societies,

132

incurred the death penalty. We read, for example, in Lev. 20. 10: "If a man commits adultery with the wife of his neighbor, both the adulterer and the adulteress shall be put to death." If a girl allowed herself to be seduced, both she and the seducer were subject to the death penalty. If, on the other hand, she was raped, only the man had to die.

As Haag has pointed out, "What is of ultimate importance in modern society in establishing the circumstances of adultery is whether one of the parties, either the man or the woman, is married. In Israel, on the other hand, what mattered was whether the woman in question was married (or betrothed). This clearly reflects the Israelite's conviction that the woman was the husband's property and that another man who seized hold of his wife was seizing hold of his property." This explains why the death penalty did not apply to a case in which a virgin who was not betrothed was seduced. What the law required in such a case was that the seducer should marry the girl (see Exod. 22. 16; Deut. 22. 28f.).

"Even today, people in the East have a much stronger sense of the social character of sexual relationships than we have in the West," Haag has claimed. "Unlike them, we tend to regard such things as a purely private matter concerning only the individuals involved."[19]

This is a clear example of the fusion of the ancient male right of possession (see above, pp. 42), the recognition of woman as a partner with equal rights and the biological ordering of relationships between partners in marriage in the interests of the group as a whole.

For a long time now, the social aspect of human sexuality has been very little stressed in Western civilization. The main emphasis has been on the individual ethical aspect. It is frequently claimed that man is able to misuse his sexual powers; it would be more correct to say that, with the help of those powers, he can misuse his fellow human beings (at least in those cases where this wrong behavior is not pathological). The consequences of this fear of misusing sexuality have certainly often been very sad, from the common assumption that to kill a human embryo is almost as bad (or equally as bad) as murder, through the division of the human body into decent and indecent parts, to the ban on birth control by inhibiting ovulation (by such means as the "pill").

Underlying this attitude and its consequences is the view that, according to the laws of nature, human sexuality and sexual partnership serve the exclusive purpose of begetting offspring. I have attempted to refute this thesis in my book on the "natural laws of marriage,"[71] in which I gave a number of examples to support my argument. The simplest of all creatures, unicellular organisms, unite sexually, but not for the purpose of multiplying. This purpose is fulfilled without sexual union by means of cellular division. Sexual intercourse takes place at certain times, but always when there is no cellular division, so that sexuality and breeding are obviously mutually exclusive.

What, then, is the biological reason for the sexual process? It is to achieve a mixture of different hereditary tendencies, to avoid genetic monotony and to increase the range of variety within the species. Many higher organisms, incuding vertebrates, procreate without sexually uniting as individuals. The newt, for example, transmits sperm indirectly and fish release sperm and eggs freely into the water. All the same, many fish practice monogamy.

There is a higher degree of certainty that a careful choice of partner some time before mating takes place will result in a better partnership. The selection is almost always better in this case than when the partners are in contact with each other for only a short time. In the latter case, there is

134

more chance that mistakes will occur and less chance of correcting them. If the partner is retained, there is as great a risk of hybridization as in the case of repeated selection of a partner. This is why the individual with a lasting partnership that is wrong is less favored by section than the individual that occasionally makes a wrong choice in repeated partnerships. Species which practice lasting monogamy therefore have an advantage over species without permanent partnership, although one sex in a species of the second group is invariaby characterized by a striking and often interchangeable display, which makes its appearance more splendid than that of the other sex. The mere fact that this is absent in the case of species which are permanently monogamous shows that this form of partnership has the same effect, that of preserving specific characteristics and avoiding hybridization.

It is therefore not difficult to see that sexual intercourse (fertilization), procreation (the preservation of the species) and sexual partnerships have different tasks to fulfill in the animal kingdom and that they can all be separated from each other. It is only of secondary importance that the act of fertilization or sexual union is connected with preserving and increasing the species, that the sexual partnership is used for the purpose of raising the young and that sexual intercourse and the care of the young are made to serve the task of forming a sexual partnership.

Species that care for their young almost always have special signals and modes of behavior which result in directing the caring actions of the parents towards the young and which draw the young to the mother and keep them near to her. In many species, these special signals and modes of behavior also have the function of bringing those of different sex together in sexual partnership. When attacked by another of the same species, some animals behave like young members of the species. They make pacifying gestures, with the result that an attitude of parental care is invoked in the aggressor, making it impossible for him to persist in attack.

Elements of this behavior, which normally have the function of establishing contact in the parents' care of the young, are also used by adults of the same species for the purpose of overcoming shyness in approaching each other. A good example of this behavior is the act of passing food from mouth to mouth. In sexual relationships, this takes place not between parent and young, but between two adult sexual partners. This happens frequently in the case of social insects, many birds, carnivores and apes. It can take the form of a greeting between partners in the act of passing food to each other or simply as a ritual greeting without passing food. In the second case, of course, the best known example is the "kiss" or beak-rubbing ritual. Other examples of elements of parental care used as approaches to the sexual partner are cleaning each other's fur—often ritualized as "delousing" or stroking—clasping each other protectively or embracing and finally making the sounds that are usually employed between mother and young of the species. These behavioral elements almost always serve only to break down shyness before copulation and therefore occur as a prelude to mating. This explains why they have often erroneously been interpreted as genuinely sexual behavior.

Begging in order to pacify an attacker is also clearly independent of hunger or the impulse to eat. In the same way, different modes of behavior that have become alienated from their original functions and have been made to serve the life of the society can also have different impulses and, from the anthropomorphic point of view, different "intentions." Yet the outward form of behavior remains the same, since the animal who receives the signal must take one "intention" for another if the behavior is to be effective.

We can go further and say that every adult animal who sees through this pacifying gesture of begging, and is not restrained from attacking because it recognizes that there is no need for parental care, fact endangers the unity and the survival of the group. This is why, in the many cases in which social signals have a twofold function of this kind, selection does not act in favor of a greater ability to differentiate between the purpose behind the signal on the part of the recipient. When an individual is not taken in by behavior which imitates that of the female or the young of the species and which furthers the communal life of the group, the life of the community is disturbed and even harmed. The advantages of the life of the society as a whole have to ensure by means of natural selection that behavior which imitates sexual approaches or parental care of the young will "please" the individual even if it is recognized to be imitative.

In addition to modes of behavior which originate as care of the young and are used to facilitate the individual's approach to a sexual partner or to another member of the group and to keep the two together, certain primarily sexual signals and elements of behavior also have the secondary function of uniting an individual to the society to which it belongs. These behavioral elements do not therefore always have an exclusively sexual intention. They may be elements belonging either to the prelude to copulation or even to the act of copulation itself. Earlier in this book, in the chapter on lying, I referred to the habit of baboons and other apes of presenting their buttocks as a pacifying gesture. Originally, of course, this is the female invitation to copulation. There is also a danger that the individual will misuse the reaction to this imitation of the female, which is necessary in order to keep the whole troop together, in order to secure an advantage for himself or to harm other members of the troop. This is also apparent in the threatening situation described in the same chapter. I have already spoken in some detail (in an earlier article)[70] about the male imitation of the signals sent as an invitation to copulation by the female baboon when she is in heat. The red buttocks which the male presents only in a social context (and never as an invitation to copulation) are originally an imitation of the bright color of the female's buttocks pads when she is in heat. The effort required for the male of a species to develop an imitation of the female's signals is the measure of the great importance of these signals to the species in question.

This also applies to the act of copulation itself, which can also act as a means of joining partners together. This is also true of human beings and, even though the Catholic Church has always been very hesitant to acknowledge the validity of modern scientific discoveries, this is something that is now officially accepted in the Church's moral teaching. If this bond between the partners and the procreation of offspring are in fact two effects of copulation which exist independently, then a special problem arises as soon as the begetting of offspring ceases to play a part in copulation and the purpose of binding the partners together is not sacrificed to the need to beget young. In this connection, it is interesting to note that a whole series of copulations, each separated from the other by a few minutes, precedes an ejaculation in the case of baboons. Each separate copulation may therefore tighten the bond between the partners, but can hardly lead to the begetting of offspring.

Many animals, either occasionally or regularly, beget more offspring than they are able to bring up, because there are, at certain times, too many individuals living in a given space with a limited supply of food. It frequently happens in such cases that signs of social stress appear before the reserves of food are exhausted, only because there is too high a density of population. This stress may have the effect of repressing sexual maturity in the young animals. What is surprising, however, is that it often does nothing to inhibit the sexual activity of the adult members of the species; instead, the offspring are destroyed.

In mice and other rodents, the fertilized ova do not become embedded in the placenta, but are immediately ejected. Even half-developed embryos are destroyed in the womb of female wild rabbits. Tree shrews under this kind of stress eat their newborn young. In most animals, the older or weaker adults succumb to symptoms of stress.

There is, then, a biological form of protection against an indiscriminate increase in the number of animals of the same species living at the same time in a region where food is limited. There are three principal means of ensuring that the population does not increase in this way. The first is to restrict the full development and the sexual maturation of some individuals. The second is to inhibit sexual behavior; and the third is to destroy embryos, newborn young and even fully grown individuals. We may therefore conclude that, whenever sexual behavior also has a social function and helps to form a bond between the partners, it is not inhibited. On the contrary, what is sacrificed is the begetting of offspring.

It is not difficult to perceive the consequences of this for man, who has gone far beyond the biological data of his life and declared the inviolability of the individual's right to live. Since the point at which the individual's existence begins can only be established arbitrarily, we may therefore think of it as beginning with the union of the germ cells. Man has, however, intervened to such an extent in his biological system that he can exercise far-reaching control over disease and other causes of death. For this reason, he is always in danger of begetting more offspring than can be borne in his environment, irrespective of limits of time and space. He cannot even allow women to have the miscarriages induced by social stress, as he knows that it is possible for him to save embryonic life by administering artificial hormones.

Yet all this does not remove social stress, but only increases it. It is completely contrary to the laws of nature and to all ethical norms to go against correct biological data and disturb the balance of a natural system by such one-sided interventions. Ultimately, this can only be harmful to man himself. The consequence is that he has had to make other, compensatory interventions. One of these is abortion, practiced with increasing frequency. Yet abortion cannot be justified either economically (because of its danger to health) or ethically.

The point at which individual human life begins has to be established, but, as I have said above, it can only be established arbitrarily. Since the individual has an inviolable right to life, ethics play an undeniable part in this arbitrarily determined point of departure. Interventions can therefore be made only in one of two ways.

The first way is to suppress sexual behavior altogether. This certainly means that there will be no offspring, but it also means that the marital relationship will be seriously impaired and even endangered. Such detrimental effects are, as we have seen, avoided in the animal kingdom.

The second way, of course, is to suppress the possibility of offspring resulting from sexual behavior. This is a typically human solution to the problem, because man is the only living creature with the necessary understanding to enable him to intervene in the natural processes at this par-

140

ticular point. What is more, the life and freedom of the individual are in no way violated. The use of what are known as artificial means of birth control is still disputed, but it can without difficulty be reconciled with biological and with ethical demands. It would clearly seem to be the most suitable solution for man's biological problems, which have been brought to light by the demands made by human ethics.

I am not claiming here that no better solutions exist, nor do I think that people can or should be officially ordered to use artificial means of preventing conception. What I do, however, believe is that a universal ban imposed on the use of these means, such as that pronounced again and again by the present pope, is without any foundation in the natural law. On the contrary, it is against all the laws of nature, even if this question is only considered within the context of the special nature of man, who is not, like the rest of creation, subject to the "earth," but who has the task of controlling it.

Equally contrary to nature is a sexual morality which does not take into account the fact that many of the elements of sexual behavior which occur in the prelude to copulation do not have the exclusive or primary function of simple sexual stimulation, but rather serve to bind the partners more closely together and to tune them more perfectly in to each other. Most of the acts of tenderness which take place before and after the sexual act itself are essential to the maintenance of a real partnership. Even though this can obviously be appreciated more easily by immediate experience than by following the less direct route of biological and ethological research, it is, I am convinced, also possible to apply ethological findings to these human questions.

The ethologist is therefore justified in criticizing many of

141

the existing ethical norms and the ancient and more recent moral commandments, both positive and negative. He is also, I believe, fully entitled to suggest, on the basis of his scientific knowledge, where and how these norms should be changed.[71]

Digression
Who Is the Pacemaker in Evolution?

THE question which inevitably arises as soon as a comparison is made between a bodily characteristic of an organism and its behavior is, which changed first in the process of evolution? Did the form of a bird's beak, for example, change first and did the bird then learn what it could best eat with that beak? Or did the bird's preference for a certain food develop first and did natural selection then favor this particular form of beak, with which the bird could best enjoy its favorite food?

The well-known psychologist, William McDougall, who died in 1938, wrote in his *Psychology, The Study of Behavior*,[40] a book that was reprinted twenty-one times between 1912 and 1945: "Progressive evolution has been primarily an evolution of mental structure and only secondarily one of bodily structure. For everywhere we find the bodily structure adapting itself to the mode of life and environment of the animal . . . The change of mode of life or of behavior leads to a change of bodily structure . . . The individuals of each generation adapt their behavior as best they can to the new environment, while the bodily structure gradually follows suit. Thus, mental evolution leads the way, and evolution of bodily structure is in the main the consequence of it."

The philosopher Herbert Spencer, whose teaching was based on the conviction that all living beings evolved, defined every stage of mental development as the expression or effect of a corresponding stage in neural evolution. These "mental" characteristics are thus made completely accessible to the ethologist and McDougall clearly took the ideas of the earlier ethologists, Saint-Hilaire and Dollo, a stage further.

Since McDougall's time, it has again and again been reaffirmed that modes of behavior are the pacemakers in evolution and that bodily structures change after the behavior has changed. When a mammal which lives on the land wants to swim, it does not first grow fins. On the contrary, it changes the coordinates of movement of the limbs that it already has. If it remains in the water, the form of these limbs will become adapted to the favored way of moving—seals and whales, in fact, have fin-like arms and legs. (I have discussed this whole question in greater detail in another book).[68] Modes of behavior which come about by means of impulse patterns of the nervous system are the instruments used to change the rigid bodily structure of the individual and adapt it to changing demands. It is not surprising that they adapt themselves more quickly to a new demand than the less flexible bodily structure.

This has consequences, however, for the establishment of ethical norms. As I have already dealt with this at length in my book on the natural laws of marriage,[71] I need only consider a few important aspects of the question here. In the case of the bedbug and other related insects, for example, the copulatory behavior of the male has developed in such a way that he no longer introduces his genitalia into those of the female, but penetrates her back. This is clearly an unnatural mode of behavior if we consider the position and the structure of the existing sexual organs of the male and female bug. In nature, however, this has not led to an elimination of this "aberration," but rather to its normaliza-

144

tion, in that the bodily structure of the female has adapted itself to this form of "extragenital" copulation. The female has evolved, on her back, at the place where the male is most expected to penetrate, a new, secondary copulatory opening of complicated structure into which the male introduces his genital organs and beneath which is a special tissue replacing the inner sexual organs and collecting the sperm.

A corresponding evolution of genital organs often takes place in the male in those parts of the body with which he usually comes into contact with the female in his attempts to approach her. For example, the male octopus uses one of his arms on which he has previously deposited the packet of sperm for the purpose of copulation. Male spiders introduce the sperm into the female genital opening with their maxillary palpi. Male guppies and swordtails, and indeed most cyprinodonts that are viviparous, have developed the first rays of their anal fins into copulatory organs and, in sharks and rays, the male sexual organ has evolved from the ventral fins. Very many and only distantly related organisms have developed a penis as an extension of the male sexual opening. Examples of this are found in many species of miller's-thumbs, in medical leeches, certain mites, harvestmen, most insects, a few birds such as the ostrich and certain ducks, in lizards and snakes and, independently from these, in tortoises, crocodiles and, of course, mammals. The structural details of the sexual organs and the modes of behavior of these organisms in mating are correspondingly different.

Since behavioral changes precede changes in bodily structure in the process of evolution, it is not possible to deduce from the bodily structure of an animal or from the form of its organs any rules as to how these organs should be used. To do so would be to subordinate the evolution of

145

behavior to that of the structure of the body. It is not possible, in other words, to argue that man had to walk upright because of the special structure of the human body. Nor is it possible to claim that it is only suitable and permissible for man to perform the sexual act in one position, that is, with the partners facing each other, because the human sexual organs are situated correspondingly.

Thus organs which eventually develop into instruments of copulation may originally have had a different function, perhaps as legs or as maxillae in the case of arthropods. In the same way, many other organs change their function and completely lose their original function in many cases. If social behavior which leads to mating favors the evolution of a penis as the organ of copulation, this male organ may also be used in all the functions in which a part is played by the behavior which originally furthered the evolution of that organ. Thus the penis of several species of free-living flat worm is also used to catch prey, because the male approaches the female as prey. Similarly, the penis of many mammals including man is also status symbol and a threatening sign.[70][71]

The biological function of modes of behavior is also able to change quite freely. Invitations to copulation can become gestures of pacification and movements to obtain food, such as begging, can become greetings. Sometimes both functions continue to be used for both purposes. The baboon's presentation of its buttocks is an invitation to copulation, but it is also—and, because it occurs so frequently, even predominantly—a gesture of submission or of pacification. The casual observer who is not aware of the difference often concludes that baboons are oversexed, regarding all the animal's gestures as sexual, when these gestures only sometimes have a sexual function.

In mammals, lactiferous glands have evolved in the sex

146

which has the most powerfully developed behavior of parental care, although they are present in an undeveloped form in the other, male sex. Once again, we see that the bodily structure follows behavior in the process of evolution.

The young mammal becomes familiar with its mother's teats not only as a source of nourishment, but also as a source of security. Young antelopes, for example, behave in this way when they are disturbed or frightened, but it is especially young apes and monkeys that run to their mothers' breasts even when they have become almost independent, not because they are hungry, but because they are in need of protection. The teats are thus clearly subject to a change in function. In certain species of ape, the mother can, as it were, "summon" her young by showing her breast. Insofar as the animal is predominantly optically orientated, this signal is more effective if the breast is very conspicuous. What is more, the female breast also has an extended social function as a signal, attracting even adult apes. The Ethiopian Gelada baboon is a particularly good example of this behavior. The breasts of the female are bright red, marked by a low décolleté of bare flesh outlined by a frill of white skin. The whole zone is thus very striking and has a clear social function. The same function is, of course, evident in human beings, although it is not the color, but the form of the human breast that is socially attractive. Many parallels and other interesting details are to be found in the animal kingdom.[71]

In this context, it is important to note that the bodily structure follows a change in function in an organ and that changes in function both in the case of organs and in that of modes of behavior are not exceptional. They are a basic principle of evolution.

If organs and modes of behavior regularly and thus with

147

sanction become alienated from their original purpose in nature, surely this principle can hardly be forbidden in the case of man, even if this alienation from the original purpose is carried out in a typically human way, with technical means. It was, after all, given to man with the primordial commandment of Genesis to subdue the earth (Gen. 1. 28). This does not, of course, mean that every form of alienation of an organ or mode of behavior is justified. What is decisive in each case is whether the aim or intention is good or evil. It cannot, however, be claimed that a freer use of sexual signals and modes of behavior, as the consequence of a changed view of partnership in marriage and in other social groupings, is necessarily either unnatural or wrong. Only those who did not understand historical evolution can insist that standards of human behavior which prevailed in the past must continue to be valid now or that a freer form of behavior might have been right in the past. As long as woman remained her husband's slave and had not become his partner, any attempt to set sexual behavior free from its purely procreative function would simply have served to foster male egoism. This, of course, still applies quite obviously to men who do not yet regard their wives as partners. More and more people now are looking for ways of making marriage a true partnership. I would suggest that a number of social signals and modes of behavior derived from biological functions, most of which were originally applied to the care of the young or to mating, could be extended to the widest variety of relationships between partners.

The Inheritance of Acquired Qualities
—Honor Your Father and Your Mother

THE rather naïve demand has been made to remove the Fourth Commandment, "Honor your father and your mother," from the Decalogue because it is the only commandment addressed, not to adults, but to children. On the other hand, the absence of a commandment "love your children" has led to the conclusion that parental care of the young is rooted in man's instincts, whereas honoring one's parents is not. Here too, there is a clear lack of understanding of the crucial biological facts which can lead to a true solution of the typically human problems included within this commandment.

This misinterpretation of the Fourth Commandment can be traced back to the false assumption that only man has a tradition. According to the Brockhaus encyclopedia, tradition is "the passing on, either orally or in writing, of knowledge and abilities, of cultural possessions and moral views to the next generation. In the case of primitive peoples, tradition is dependent on direct imitation and memory." Oral or written tradition, of course, points directly to speech, but the reference to direct imitation shows that speech can be dispensed with. What is more, speech is not only dispensable in the case of primitive peoples, as Brockhaus suggests. In more developed societies, many insignificant traditional details are taken over from the parents, without the use of speech or concepts. Furthermore, the

149

passing on of knowledge and abilities is also usual among individuals belonging to the same generation, so that it sometimes happens that the older generation learns something from the younger generation and then passes it on. As there is, to my knowledge, no special term for this process, I include it within the category of tradition, which is therefore, according to this conception, not tied to a minimal age difference between the individual handing on the information and the one receiving it.

Living organisms learn to store their experiences in memory in order to put them to use later. It is clear, then, that the loss of these experiences and their practical application with the death of the individual is a great disadvantage to the species as a whole, with the result that the experiences are collected and handed on, in the same way as information transmitted by heredity is of advantage to the species. I have no need to add to the great amount that has already been written about the parallel between tradition and heredity elsewhere.[53] I am, however, bound to say that new experiences are disseminated with far greater speed among the population of a given species through the channel of tradition than by the process of heredity. An inherited characteristic can be passed on only as quickly as the whole organism can be procreated, whereas a traditionally acquired quality can be passed on to many or even to all members of the population at the same time, according to the degree of perfection achieved in the means of communication. In the competition between tradition and heredity that takes place in the process of gaining and assimilating information, tradition is highly successful. In the juristical sense, not in the biological and eugenetical sense, of the word "inheritance," tradition creates the possibility of inheriting acquired qualities and abilities.

The new individual member of a species of necessity

acquires hereditary characteristics when it acquires life. It cannot avoid acquiring them. By simply learning nothing at all, it can, on the other hand, avoid acquiring traditional qualities. Hereditary peculiarities are transmitted and extended by procreation, but traditional characteristics are handed on only if there are others in the wake of the first recipient trying to acquire the new quality. This desire for new experience is dependent on curiosity, without which it would be impossible for anything new or different to be learned.

There is, however, a difference between learning from experience and learning from others. In the first case, the individual has itself to collect experience from the object. In the second case, it receives experiences from a store of information, namely, the memory of another individual. Apart from the possibility of error which is always present, what has been learned from the object will undoubtedly fit the object, in other words, it will be correct. What is traditionally learned from others, on the other hand, may be wrong—it need not necessarily fit the object. It is quite possible for behavior that has become completely meaningless to be handed on traditionally. It is only when information has been gained from a store, that is, from heredity or from memory and its technical offshoots, that historical remnants can be formed and collected as historical ballast.[68] [69]

It is, moreover, only by examining historical remnants of this kind that are common to two or more species that the research worker can tell with any certainty which organisms are related to each and how closely they are related. This would not be possible if they were all ideally suited to present-day needs. The ethologist specializing in the study of homologies can, for example, deduce from historical remnants that two individuals have the same origin and descent. The same specialist can also investigate the affinities of tradition by means of these historical remnants and can in this way make a very important contribution to ethology by reconstructing the development of social norms.

It is an indisputable fact that animals can traditionally hand on knowledge and abilities that they have acquired individually. Perhaps the most obvious example of this is that most (though by no means all!) young songbirds learn to sing from their parents (usually from the father alone). Young birds raised in captivity by man often learn tunes that are whistled to them again and again and are able to pass these on to their young.

The European green finch (*Chloris chloris*) frequently eats the seeds of the mezereon (*Daphne mezereum*), a shrub cultivated as a garden plant in England because of its flowers. As soon as the seeds are ripe, the green finches fly down into the bush and strip it of seeds. There is considerable evidence that this eating habit of the green finch originally occurred once, and only once, about a hundred or two hundred years ago in the Pennines. It then spread, by tradition, into the north and the south of England at the rate of about one and a quarter to two and a half miles annually.[63]

Observations have been made with captive ravens and it has been established that one raven will invent a game which the other ravens in the same aviary will quickly learn from him, whereas ravens in other aviaries will not.[18] This shows clearly enough that what is acquired traditionally is not always restricted exclusively to skills that are absolutely necessary for survival.

Particularly good examples of what may be called "precultural" traditions have been provided by the Japanese in their researches into the macaque *Macaca fuscata*, a Japanese relation of the rhesus monkey.[45][59] In the autumn of

152

1953, the female Japanese macaque Imo, who was eighteen months old at the time, washed dirty sweet potatoes or batatas (the tubers of a member of the convolvulus family) in the water of a stream before eating them. This drew the attention of ethologists to the little island of Kôshima to the south of Kyushu. One month later, one of Imo's playmates also began to wash sweet potatoes. Four months later, Imo's mother was also doing it. The practice spread more and more through daily contact between mothers and children, companions and playmates. By 1957, fifteen of the sixty monkeys in the group were washing batatas. In the next five years, the practice that had originated with Imo had spread further, above all because mothers were instructing their young to wash the roots. By 1962, forty-two of the total group of fifty-nine monkeys were able to do it. Within ten years, the practice of washing sweet potatoes that one young monkey had invented had become the usual eating behavior of almost the whole of this community of macaques.

Other groups of the same species of macaque have different traditions. One troop likes to eat eggs, another does not. One troop living on Mount Atoga near Tokyo will not touch rice or soya beans, whereas another troop elsewhere causes great damage in the paddy field and among the soya crops.

The special "gift" or learning ability that underlies the assimilation of such traditions differs remarkably from troop to troop and from individual to individual. A troop from Mount Takasaki, for example, learned very slowly, whereas another troop from Mount Minu near Osaka learned especially quickly. Six of the seven children of the female macaque Nami from the batata-washing troop never learned to wash batatas and were shown in various tests to be less gifted.

On the other hand, Imo, who had first learned to wash sweet potatoes in 1953, also discovered in 1956 the "gold-washing process." Instead of doing what had always been done by the members of the troop before and laboriously picking up grains of corn individually out of the sand where they had been scattered, Imo one day took the mixture of sand and corn in her hands and threw it into the water, where the sand sank to the bottom. Although this might have been obvious to all the monkeys that had already been putting sweet potatoes into the water, this practice also spread in the same way, by social contact, and once again very slowly. By 1962, nineteen monkeys in the troop were using this process.

An invention of this kind readily draws other, similar inventions in its wake. At first, the Japanese macaques washed their sweet potatoes in the fresh water of a stream. Later, they washed them on the beach and, since 1962, they have been using more and more salt water, dipping the tubers that they have already nibbled again and again into the sea while they are eating and thus making their food more palatable.

The corn-washing macaques, who went to the water with their hands full of corn and sand, learned to walk upright on their hind legs for quite long distances and to stand upright while they were washing the corn. They also found other things to eat in the water when the tide had gone out and collected them. Later they learned to swim and even dive quite well, so that they were able to find food in the sea when the water was high. The female macaque Eba and her daughter Sango never washed corn themselves, but formed a band and attacked others as soon as they had thrown their corn into the water to wash it.

Ways of preparing and acquiring food were not the only forms of behavior that were discovered and handed on

154

traditionally to other individuals, however. The same process also took place in the case of certain rules of social behavior, for example, attention or indifference on the part of males with regard to females who were not in heat and the role of babysitter and protector of the young played by males with a high rank in the hierarchy. Generally speaking, males of low rank are not allowed to eat in the vicinity of a male of high rank, but in one group they ate regularly side by side "at the same table." Again, as a rule, young males are almost always banished from the close company of males occupying a higher position in the group and their females. In one particular group, however, they were permitted to mix with the females. In many groups, the males only mount the females for the purpose of copulating, but in one group mounting took place frequently without any direct sexual connotation. It is clear, then, from these examples that the pattern of social life may to a great extent be regulated by tradition in the animal kingdom.

When a discovery by one member of a species is extended to others, what is most striking is how slowly this process of handing-on takes place. A purposeful form of instruction hardly exists at all, although, in many animals, the mothers give additional emphasis, by means of special modes of behavior, to the techniques of electing and catching prey, with the result that it is relatively easy for the young to acquire both of these techniques.

On the other hand, however, there are limits to this extension of a discovery. In the case of the Japanese macaques that learned to wash sweet potatoes, only eighty per cent of the monkeys in the troop had acquired this skill after the first ten years of observation. The remaining twenty per cent consisted mainly of very young infants and old males of high rank in the troop. "Ultraconservative" old macaques, completely refusing to wash batatas, were living

155

BIOLOGY OF THE TEN COMMANDMENTS

side by side with "progressive" young monkeys who washed
the tubers independently, having learned it from their
mothers.

There is a special biological reason for this difference
between the generations. When the possibility exists for the
handing on of experiences, it is extremely important not
only for new experiences to be collected, but also for them
to be conserved. Such experiences are automatically collected by the one who has them and, moreover, they accumulate with time and increasing age. The older he is, the
more experienced he becomes and the more he has to con-
serve.

In a society of younger and older animals, this inevitably
results in a division of functions. The older members of the
group have the task of conserving experiences, whereas the
younger, less "prejudiced" animals have to collect new
experiences. As a consequence of this division of tasks,
youth has to give free rein to curiosity and experimentation,
while age specializes in conservation and persistence, so
that learning new skills becomes more difficult with increasing age and rank. This is a biological necessity whenever
experiences are both collected and conserved in an animal
society.

This situation can only be changed when an organism
discovers how to hand on experiences in symbolic language.
All tradition is conveyed in the animal kingdom by means
of "objects." Both the transmitter and the recipient of
tradition must encounter the object to which the experience
is related at the same time if the skill is to be conveyed by
the experienced animal to another member of the species.
It is only by means of demonstrations carried out with or in
the presence of the enemy, for example, the prey, the food
or the way of dealing with it that these objects can be
learned by organisms without a spoken or written language.
If sweet potatoes are not available to a whole generation of

Japanese macaques, for example, the tradition of washing them will disappear.

Man, on the other hand, is able to describe, with the help of symbols, not only an object but also the most suitable way of associating with that object and to hand on that description to other men. It is clear, of course, that man learns very many of his skills simply by looking and imitating more experienced fellow men, so that we may conclude that handing on by means of objects plays a very important part in tradition in his case. Nonetheless, his tradition is also to a very great extent conveyed symbolically.

Even in his task of handing on traditional knowledge, information and skills by teaching, however, man can be replaced by written or recorded material, books and teaching machines. The use of such methods relieves older members of the human community of their function as living storehouses of experience and allows them to interrelate their various experiences, to test their knowledge by correlative methods, to establish cross-connections between data which point to natural laws and cannot be discovered without a process of abstraction.

This type of research is all the more likely to succeed if those engaged in it have a full, wide and varied experience. One discovery that has been made in this connection is that traditions and rules of behavior are inevitably adapted to conditions of time, place and circumstance. They are bound to change when these circumstances change or when the organisms themselves change. An example of this is the behavior of the Australian aborigines mentioned earlier in this book—each tribe is right to behave as it does in its own territory and its rules cannot be transferred to any other conditions. If this principle is clearly understood, it should be possible to overcome group hatred.

Man's astonishing technical development is, of course,

157

the result of this systemization, which is in turn based on the use of symbols and storehouses of information that are not restricted to individuals. This is precisely what distinguishes human tradition from all the traditions that have so far been discovered in the animal kingdom, with one very important exception. With the help of special movements, the honeybees responsible for collecting are able to report to each other in the hive the distance, direction and productivity of a source of food. What is more, they do not transfer the experience that they have acquired to others in the hive by means of the object, but by symbols. This experience, however, is passed on by means of symbols only from one bee to a second bee. So far, no bee has been observed to hand on the information that it has received from another bee at once and directly to a third member of the community. The second bee simply flies directly to the source of food about which it has been informed by the first bee, collects it and then, on its return, informs a third bee. In this way, the system is insured against "rumors." This seems to be very effective in the case of organisms such as bees, which are unable to evaluate different reports against each other, when, for example, different collectors report good supplies obtainable at different places. If, in other words, the individual cannot decide which of several different traditions is the most useful to him, it is clearly better for him to be spared this conflict. This is always possible as long as all the others from whom the individual learns have the same background of tradition as he does and as long as he does not come into contact with others of a different tradition. This explains why animals only learn, often with surprising obstinacy, from members of the same species that they know. This mutual knowledge is the guarantee that they all belong to the right group.

(This process can be partly explained by using the

158

radically simplified analogy of a German married to an Englishwoman, both of whom are teaching their son to drive. The German teaches the son to drive on the right, the English wife teaches him to drive on the left, according to the country in which they are staying at the time. In Germany, the wife is silent about the rules of driving, in England, the husband keeps quiet. They do this until their son is capable of knowing that neither of the two ways of driving is absolutely right, but that each is right according to the place. Eventually, the learner understands that he cannot drive on the right or the left both in Germany and England, but that he has to apply one or other rule according to the circumstances.)

I have already stressed several times that information and skills traditionally transmitted are placed at the service of the group's adaptation to the environment and therefore play an important part in the survival of the group. Knowledge and skills, which differ from group to group, provide each group with an ecological niche which is relatively free from competition and within which each group can develop. It is therefore advantageous from the point of view of evolution if different traditions are kept quite distinct. This is possible if the recipients of traditional knowledge and skills are protected against the inflow of traditions which are alien to the group. Whenever an understanding of the connections between systems exists, however, the knowledge and abilities of other groups can be used, in which case it is more advantageous to have a store of as many skills as possible which can be applied to all the environmental conditions that might occur. Here the organisms of the group become not so much specialists as universal specialists.

Organisms gifted with this understanding will inevitably try to acquire the inventions made by other groups. This results in a competition for other traditions which had not previously existed and which compels every group to protect itself, by concealment, secrecy or other means, including even "patenting" its inventions, against an outflow of traditions to other groups. An additional fact that has to be taken into account is the well-known selective principle that information is most successfully accumulated if it is multiplied. The hereditary factors which are present in most offspring are those which prevail and precisely the same applies to the doctrines which are accepted by most individuals. These are spread not by procreation, like heredity, but by conviction. For this reason, "selection by success" favors all attempts at conversion which may increase the number of individuals following one's own doctrine at the expense of those following another. In such cases, doctrines compete with each other like parties for members.

It is, of course, true that it is only possible to deal with the disadvantages to human society and to classes of men and nations which result from this process by tolerance, a tolerance which can be identified, at least partly, with love of one's fellow men. It is often forgotten that neither tolerance nor active love of one's neighbor come about automatically. The exercise of both is dependent on a conscious renunciation of competition for other ideas as well as for followers of one's own. The least that can be done in this case is to assess objectively the value and suitability of such ideas, doctrines, skills and elements of information and knowledge. These ideas and doctrines should, in other words, not be judged according to the number of people who believe in them. A comparison with the animal kingdom should help us to see how much importance to attach to this.

The part played by experienced older members of animal societies has been widely recognized, especially in the case of apes and monkeys. In any troop of baboons, the members with the highest rank and enjoying priority with regard to food and females in heat are, of course, the most powerful mature males. Yet almost every troop contains, in addition to these high-ranking males, a number of almost toothless old baboons. These old apes are for the most part simply fellow travelers. They do not compete with other members of the troop, who, on the other hand, do not try to take advantage of them or expel them. It is possible that the recognition of property, which I have already discussed in a previous chapter, plays a part here.

In most situations, the most powerful males are the leaders of the troop. They decide where to go in search of food in the morning and they choose which path the troop will follow in the evening to reach shelter for the night. If, however, something unexpected is encountered on the way home, something that gives rise to doubts, or if there has been a sudden heavy shower, flooding all the paths that are known to the leaders and blocking them, the leaders simply sit down and, as it were, place their authority at the disposal of others. What happens again and again in such cases is that the old apes take the lead and, making use of their experience, choose a path or a détour which the younger males did not know. The rest of the troop follows these older, experienced baboons as they had previously followed the leaders.[29]

It is not only baboons that keep the old, experienced members of the troop in reserve as a "council of wise men." Many primitive peoples do exactly the same—the Bushmen,[58] the Australian aborigines,[12] the Eskimos[16] and the Tibetans, who have special songs which emphasize the need to treat old people with respect in view of their wisdom and experience.[21] Similarly, the Fourth Commandment of the Decalogue does not require us to *love* our parents or old people, but to *honor* them. The Hebrew verb used in the

161

Old Testament for "to honor" is *kabēd*. This verb only occurs in connection with persons and things with a sacral character, such as the angel of Yahweh, the king, Jerusalem, the Temple, the Sabbath or the wise man.[19]

The Bushmen make a clear distinction between "rank" and "reputation." Rank depends on the office that a person assumes. That person's reputation depends on the way in which he carries out the office. When ethologists use the words "rank" and "order of rank," they often overlook this distinction. The reputation of individual elephants, apes and wild dogs, as well as other vertebrates, is often connected with their role—the best hunter or guard is not always the best babysitter. In the case of the Bushmen, the most successful hunter always enjoys the highest reputation and has the last word in all matters concerned with hunting. In other matters, his opinion can be deliberately ignored. His reputation does not, however, depend solely on definite technical skills or achievements, but on his personality and his character as well. That is, it depends on how he succeeds in making his opinion prevail and how he approaches other members of the community. It also depends on whether he has a sense of humor and can bear being teased.[58] The authority that an individual has in the community is determined by "public opinion." It is not in the first place an "authority of office" which he claims for himself, but an authority which is granted to him by the other members of the community. The distinction is the same as that between property that is claimed and property that is recognized by others. Social authority is, in fact, a kind of property.

Authority that is recognized and given by others is democratic, but it is biologically meaningful only if public opinion is formed objectively and with regard to the opinion of the individual and individual specialized groups. Modern

162

society is becoming more and more functionally specialized and this is leading to an increasing diversity of individual opinions concerning the choice of leaders in different spheres of activity. Decisions have to be taken by representatives of all these functions.

This phenomenon can be observed in a society of bees. The choice of a new location for a swarm of bees is not made merely by the collectors jointly. On the contrary, the advice of expert counselors is sought, the so-called "scouts," and after each of these gathers information about the different places available, the final decision rests with them.

On the other hand, however, those who are entitled to vote ought to have the opportunity of testing the fitness of the leader in question. In other words, authority has to be justified. This is customary in man's everyday life. The reputation of a good midwife may, for example, be much higher than that of a doctor in general practice. Again, if a man suddenly stops in the street, makes excited gestures and announces loudly that he knows how to ensure world peace and that all people have to do is to follow him, the public would undoubtedly insist first of all that his mental state be examined. This does not mean that he may not be right in the end. What has to be established at first is whether he is right to claim authority and to be followed. Leaving malice on one side, the more chance there is of mistakes being made, the more important it is to test an authority critically. If this were always done, it would not be possible for one person who really knows better, but whom the others do not recognize, to prevail against the others and compel them to accept the happiness or prosperity that he plans for them. Tolerance cannot be spread by means of intolerance. Whenever this happens, it is a victory for intolerance.

What I have suggested in the foregoing paragraphs may

perhaps point to the way along which we can begin to look for the biological laws governing human societies and for the help we may gain from comparisons with animal societies. The commandment, to honor age is quite clearly connected with the formation of tradition and the accumulation of experience. It is also possible to understand, in this perspective, the much discussed promise that is appended to the commandment to honor age, "that your days may be long (and that it may go well with you) in the land which the Lord your God gives you" (Exod. 21. 12; Deut. 5. 16). This is one biological consequence that is also visible in societies which are not human. The other consequence, which is less well known, but which is equally important biologically is this: Authority has to be justified and, quite apart from whether it is right or wrong, it does not have to be followed if it cannot be justified.

PART 3

Some Biological and Ethical Conclusions

As far as I am able to judge, the ethologist's attempt to trace the basic ethical demands made on man and human society back to a biological origin is fully justified, both from the biological and from the ethical point of view. After all, "tracing back" should not be confused with "deducing from." They are different processes. Anyone can trace his origin and that of his near and more distant relatives back to certain ancestors. What he cannot do is to deduce descendants from given ancestors. If this were possible, he would be able to predict his own grandchildren. Only the past can be reconstructed, not the future.

This applies as well to comparative biology and to the use of comparative methods in ethology, which do not permit us to deduce human characteristics from those of animals, but which do enable us to trace them back to animal behavior. In so doing, we are able to learn about the way in which such qualities and characteristics evolve and even, if a sufficient number of parallel cases is studied, how qualities and characteristics in certain categories usually evolve. When such laws are known, we can to some extent predict possible and probable developments and at the same time apply these laws to give direction to this further development.

Again and again one encounters qualities and characteristics which occur at a certain stage of evolution and which cannot be traced back to earlier stages, although

167

they are composed of parts that were present at an earlier period. Every system of rules consists of such elements, yet the circle of rules has no preliminary stages—either deviations between the existing situation and the optimum are corrected or they are not. We cannot, however, discover which human characteristics cannot be traced back to previous stages of evolution outside the human sphere merely by pious wishes. Only detailed and precise research will provide an answer to this question. What interests us here are those characteristics of human behavior which are required—or forbidden—by universally recognized commandments and which can be compared with corresponding behavioral characteristics in other living organisms.

"The first commandment of any ethos of penal law must be that no threat of punishment should be permitted if it is not in some clearly recognizable way related to ensuring survival, to the fundamental demand of biological existence, to the tangible legal endowments that are necessary if this demand is to be fulfilled and to the exclusion of violence or insidiousness." These words were spoken by Adolf Arndt when he addressed the forty-seventh assembly of German jurists in 1968. It is clear from this that jurists are also aware of the primacy of the biological demand that the species should be preserved. As we have seen, the inviolability of the individual is required in addition to this prehuman demand, as a typical human demand and as the central problem of the commandments discussed here. This individual inviolability is made problematical by the way in which our "neighbor" or fellow man is usually defined and, even within this definition, there is often a norm, from which many people feel compelled to depart because of the prevailing circumstances. Certain nomadic peoples, for example, must on occasion kill children or expose their old people and let them die. Other peoples, who are never

168

compelled to resort to these practices, often regard themselves, for this reason, as morally better. (It may be noted that much of the aversion that settled peoples have to nomads seems to go back to these practices.)

Different social systems can continue to exist alongside each other as long as they remain isolated from each other. The more people of different origins and with different traditions and ways of life come into contact with each other, however, the more homogeneous the various systems of interhuman relationships become. A selection operates against the less adaptive systems among prevailing relationships in this process and those favored by selection try to convert those who follow other systems. In this, they have to take care that the result will not be the triumph of a particular social system, but rather an improvement in living conditions for other people.

Even the man who bears this in mind, however, has still to be constantly and indeed increasingly alert to the functional structure and the biological limits of interhuman relationships, because man's ability consciously to plan and shape the future also implies a duty. He has a duty to investigate the way of life not only of other peoples, but also of his own group. Even development aid which functions particularly well inevitably gives rise to problems for those who benefit from that aid. Research into the future of man in society, which is now still at its beginning stages, has therefore to take seriously into account the functional and biological laws of human societies in order to help man to foresee and thus to avoid the undesirable side-effects of the changes that he is planning.

The Indians living in the Paraguayan part of the Mato Grosso have, since time immemorial, been preparing a very effective birth control tea from the dried leaves and stems of the plant *Stevia rebaudiana*. In any attempt to prevent them

169

from using this means of contraception, for whatever reason, the possible side-effects must be taken into account. The Indians themselves would be forbidden to follow such directions if they knew that they emanated from Western Europe, where every second baby is unintentionally conceived by its parents. People and groups claiming authority have to justify themselves by expert knowledge. What is alien and uncontrollable has to be rejected, not simply defamed. This is, from the biological point of view, only reasonable and it is only in this way that human societies can preserve an adaptive pluriformity.

Again, from the biological point of view, it is quite unreasonable to normalize all qualities, characteristics, values and individual differences. The much-vaunted ideal of universal equality is only reasonable if it is related to something which all men have in common, something in respect of which individual human differences are quite irrelevant and play no part at all. Research into the natural range of diversity in human modes of behavior and talents ought therefore to enable us to see the essentially human element much more clearly. Differences are necessary for the purpose of comparison, but they are eliminated when everything is made equal and leveled down. Here too, it is possible for biology to help us to verify our thinking. Generalizations such as "beavers are monogamous" often conceal a typical error in thinking, namely that all non-monogamous adult beavers are somehow unsuccessful in their natural aim. In fact, however, there are in nature many variations maintained by special mechanisms which result in distinct advantages to the species in question. Our first question, then, should be this: do individuals who deviate from the norm not perhaps bring certain advantages to the species as a whole? (A good example of this phenomenon are the worker and soldier classes of social insects, which

170

depart from the norm in that they are sterile. The species as a whole derives distinct advantages from these members of the species which deviate from the norm.)

The attempt to approach the problem of human norms from the vantage point of biology is not always successful; it is only by making the attempt that we can ascertain whether it will succeed or not. It would certainly be wrong to assume that whatever is not forbidden in nature or by instinct will not be forbidden in civilization or by tabu. This is clear from the commandment not to kill others, which extends far beyond man himself in the form of very varied instinctive inhibitions against killing. (These are probably also present in man himself.) This does not mean, however, that all tabus have to be traced back to instinctive inhibitions. This would undoubtedly be difficult to do in the case of the frequently encountered tabu against eating a totem animal. In discussing this, my aim has above all been to show that my attempted interpretation does not claim to be the magic button. I am, however, convinced that it is necessary and that it is fully justified.

THE EVOLUTION OF NORMS

Normal behavior differs according to place, time and circumstance. An obvious example of this is that smacking one's lips and belching while eating is regarded as a polite acknowledgment of one's appreciation of a good meal in many places, but is tabu in the West, where we praise the person who has prepared the meal verbally. Another example is the difference between the polite behavior of the dock worker and that of the company director. The Ten Commandments are, of course, more than merely polite formulae, but there are parallels between them in the differ-

171

ent ways in which they are interpreted. To enumerate these would inevitably lead to misunderstandings. In any case, I am not concerned in this book so much with what is normal in the sense of what occurs most frequently—with the numerical norm, in other words—as with the aim, orientation or direction of behavior as a norm. It would therefore be better to use the word "direction" rather than "norm," as this would emphasize that an aim is involved and that the direction changes according to the position occupied by the recipient, even if the aim is the same in every case.

In his exposition of the *hexaemeron* or six days of creation, Augustine argued that, when God rested on the seventh day from his work and saw that it was good, everything was indeed finished and had to stay like that, because any further change could only be the consequence of sin. Even now, eminent authors are afraid, as Augustine was fifteen centuries ago, that an acceptance of "progress" and a "new" morality will open the way for what D. von Hildebrand has called "the Trojan horse in the City of God."[22]

But do he and others like him really believe that the city of God is so unstable? Erik Erikson recently affirmed that we can no longer allow ourselves the luxury of history as we have known it in the past. But simply to wait for what happens to us, to be resigned, in other words, to "God's will," is in contradiction to the task given to us in Genesis to "subdue" the earth.

Of course, traditions change gradually as time passes, but this change is often far too slow. I have already discussed the biological reasons for this. But as soon as radical deviations from the accepted norm appear in the daily activity of whole groups of men and women, accompanied by a continued opposition to any change in the way in which these norms are expressed, evolution parts company with these norms, or rather directions, causing them to lose their value as pointers. We do not, however, have to wait until these traditional norms change of their own accord. On the contrary, we have to be active in changing them ourselves and, to do this properly, we have to understand, at least to some extent, the structure of human behavior and its norms.

Many ethologists hope that their work will contribute to that understanding of human behavior by revealing its biological foundations. This leads many pessimists to conclude that human behavior cannot be changed because it is based on natural laws. They might be right if we were simply unable or unwilling to take any action. They may even believe that human freedom is an illusion because human behavior has its origins in natural laws and perhaps even in the laws of evolution. Why, then, do they not simply give up the task of educating their children and stop giving good advice to others? After all, the prerequisite for both of these activities is that they shall have an effect on others. Both too are a stage in human evolution. In doing more than simply handing on our own experience, in trying to ensure that our children enjoy a better and fuller life than we do, we are looking forward to further evolution and encouraging the growth of tradition and norms.

This will, of course, quite often entail the emergence of discrepancies in the prevailing tradition and in the currently valid norms. But the uneasiness that is caused by these discrepancies acts as a brake on any tendency to abandon a norm too readily, even though it need not and should not in fact make it difficult or impossible for us to take action against the valid norm. This has to be accepted as part of the bargain. This is something that is clearly revealed in the Catholic doctrine of *epikeia*. This doctrine, that of the decision based on fairness, affirms that a law may not be applicable in certain cases; this depends on the deeper meaning or intention of the legislator.

Epikeia is a moral attitude which is directed towards what is objectively demanded and what is in accordance with the prevailing situation. The Catholic Church includes *epikeia* among the fundamental Christian virtues, although, for various reasons, the doctrine is not widely publicized in the Church. It is, however, completely in accordance with what the biologist knows about man and the demands that he makes as a result of this knowledge.

I hope it is quite clear that this is completely different from what is usually known as situational ethics, which I regard as a pseudoethical attempt to gloss over or excuse any and every action to suit one's own convenience. After all, the more interconnections between various actions that we have to bear in mind, the less we are left to our own discretion or convenience.

BALANCED SYSTEMS AND OPTIMUM NORMS

In any attempt to evaluate human behavior ethically on a basis of biology, we are at once confronted with a basic problem which has so far not been solved and which is responsible for many human difficulties.

Our naïve norm of "good—bad" is one-dimensional and based on extreme values. The more a man loves his neighbor, the better he is—the less love he has for his neighbor, the worse he is; the more obedient he is, the better he will behave—the less obedient, the less well behaved; the more he seeks after pleasure, the worse it is for him—the less pleasure he seeks, the better.

Most biological processes, on the contrary, take place according to adaptive mean values which become less adaptive as they tend towards one extreme or another. The temperature of the human body, for example, does not become better the higher it rises. The optimum is 37°C (98.6°F.) and deviations either above or below this norm are dangerous. The same applies to other physiological factors. This is generally accepted in the case of the consumption of food. It is also true, though not universally acknowledged, in the case of man's procreation of offspring. It is also so in his need of sleep and in his need to place himself in a superior or an inferior position with regard to others. The norms that are required, then, are not orientated towards extremes, but towards an optimum.

Optimum curves, falling off at each end, come about as a result of opposing processes which are in a state of equilibrium with each other. Psychiatrists are of the opinion nowadays, for example, that masturbation among young people, which in the past led to almost grotesque countermeasures by adults, is a normal traditional stage on the way to individual maturity and that to masturbate too little is perhaps as dangerous as to do it too much.

Although this opinion may be challenged from the biological point of view, it can act as quite a suitable model. The impulse to masturbate may lead to an experience of oneself and then make experience in sexual partnership possible. The fact that others disapprove may also act as a movement in the opposite direction and prevent this experience from developing into a harmful and self-centered extreme. If both of these tendencies take place, even grotesque countermeasures would be justifiable so long as it could be shown that they are not one hundred per cent successful, in other words, that they do not reduce behavior to a level below the optimum.

Many educational measures are so constituted that they cannot be made perfect; others, on the other hand, can be perfected, in which case it is important to know how the system to be regulated functions. The very least of the

175

current ways of evaluating ethical behavior seem to me to be equal to the demands made by a norm orientated towards an optimum. As long as we are unable to define the connections between the various biological systems quantitatively, we shall not be able to calculate the optimum values, but shall simply have to try them out in practice. In this case, all that we can be sure of is that we cannot simply continue as we like in the same direction, even if the result is at first favorable. This is because we are bound to encounter at some point the optimum, although we shall not recognize it until we have gone beyond it. It is, in other words, not possible to stop at exactly the right time if the place where the optimum is situated is not known in advance. We shall inevitably stop too soon or too late. As soon as one reaches the top of a hill, one begins to go down the other side.

The very lack of biological and other data means that we are still at the experimental stage in establishing norms. A striking characteristic of this stage is that corrective measures allow the biological system to move backwards and forwards across a supposed optimum. Although this optimum acts like the neutral position of a swinging pendulum and is crossed again and again from both sides, it is nonetheless much shorter in extent than the deviations from the norm.

All biological systems, including societies, are equilibrium systems and all man's interventions into these systems which have produced undesirable consequences have failed to take this question into account. It is simply not true, for example, that long-range weapons release man's aggressive urge more powerfully, with the result that the inhibiting mechanisms that prevent him from killing his fellow men are no longer effective. It is not the technique of the weapons employed that is to blame for this behavior, but

176

the imbalanced application of the technique, which increases only the range of the weapons and not the range over which their effects can be reported back and imagined (something which would be quite possible to do).

It has been repeatedly stressed that the soldiers who are directly involved in a war fight more as a consequence of obedience to their authorities than from personal hostility towards the enemy. The politicians who begin a war or who intervene in it are also not usually personally aggressive towards those whom their country is fighting. It would seem, then, that the causes of war, which is often put forward as a suitable example of human aggression on a large scale, are to be found above all in an imbalance in the relationship between the beginnings and the consequences, between submission to and control of authorities in society. The problem existed long before the development of modern weapons. It is regrettable that so little use has been made in this context to date of the very penetrating and informative studies that have been made of tribal wars, their beginnings and consequences—for example, among the Papuans of New Guinea[39] and the Amazon Indians.[3] Although the customs and morals of these two groups developed quite independently of each other, they show very remarkable parallels.

Many animals which grow up in family societies, such as geese, rabbits and monkeys, are helped in quarrels by their relatives. The young of these species are socially successful not only because of their own efforts, but also because of the effective protection given to them by others. What we have here, then, is the unsolved problem of the traditional hierarchy of rank and of official authority, which is not the consequence of the animal's own performance. We still do not know how these animals test their potential leaders or how they remove incapable ones.

177

Man is faced again and again with this problem and with the need to solve it. This should encourage him to examine biological models. Closely connected with the selection of leaders and with the need to control the way in which they carry out their function is the link between rank and age and the link between age and ability. Any system for evaluating leaders which is based on biological relationships and which therefore allows rank to rise automatically with an increase in the number of years of service, as in the case of baboons, must eventually suffer from imbalance. This is obvious if we consider the increasing success in modern medicine in extending man's expectation of life, but its corresponding failure to guarantee an increased performance. The imbalance, in other words, results from the fact that the optimum performance precedes the maximum expectation of life. It hardly needs to be stressed that this concerns not only the leaders, but also those who follow them.

The many undesirable social side-effects that have resulted from man's increased expectation of life and the greatly diminished rate of infant mortality are well enough known, although we do not always know how to deal with these side-effects. Doctors who simply adhere to the Hippocratic oath and who dismiss all methods of preventing conception as basically contrary to medical ethics (because birth control is directed towards the prevention of life and not towards its preservation) forget one very important factor: all the living systems entrusted to his care are equilibrium systems, in which one element can be changed only to a certain extent before other elements are also affected. It is contrary to biological law (and unfair to the Creator) to interfere with a living system and to upset its balance intentionally and even with a good intention and then to burden the natural law with all the disturbing side-effects that may subsequently appear.

178

As world population grows, so too does the problem of obtaining food. (Some people are naïve enough to think that all that has to be done is to open up and develop all the reserves of food for the population of the world to be able to increase to unlimited numbers.) Food, however, is only one problem; there is also the problem of the division of living space in a world population of increasing density. Density stress becomes urgent even before a shortage of food makes itself felt, and the distance between individuals, the defense of individual and group territories and similar behavioral characteristics call for immediate attention as important subjects for intensive research.

The greater the number of individuals living together in a restricted space, the more anonymous their social life becomes. Animals living together in small groups know each other individually. The thousands of individuals living in an insect state only identify each other anonymously by the scent that is characteristic for the state. The behavior mechanisms that have to be used to regulate society in such large groups, then, are those which act anonymously and which are based not on individual, but on supraindividual means of communication. In animal societies, the relationship between individual partners may be sacrificed to this. In human societies, the prevailing opinion is that they should be preserved if at all possible. The mechanisms binding members of the same species together anonymously are also effective in binding individual partners together. I have already drawn attention to the fact that modes of behavior and signals related to parental care of the young which have become alienated from their original purpose are used to bind sexual partners together. The same social signals and modes of behavior may also serve the purpose of anonymously binding together individuals who are completely unknown to each other. The significance of this be-

179

havior may therefore vary according to whether it occurs between individuals who know each other or between individuals who do not know each other. In either case it can be biologically advantageous. The more frequently anonymous contacts occur, the more the "public" behavior that is accepted as normal must be changed by these contacts.

This anonymity also has other side-effects, however. A Bushman who has committed a crime is expelled from the group and is therefore to a great extent isolated, because he is known to everyone and everyone learns about his expulsion. In a large town, on the other hand, a criminal simply merges into the large anonymous group because he can best hide where he is not conspicuous as an individual, and where he is unknown.

I have tried to give a few indications of the existing biological and functional networks of effects and demands. The commandments that I have discussed in this book are clearly those which deal with those aspects of social life that are urgently in need of regulation and control. Any attempt to regulate one of these aspects will also have an effect on all the other interrelated aspects. Once we have some insight into the nature of the biological foundations of the individual commandments, the next step is to examine the biological connections between these foundations. It hardly needs to be stressed, of course, that we cannot wait until we have completed our research into these biological foundations before beginning to take action in the sphere of human social life, including that of the education of children. The inevitable consequence of this is that we are now in all probability using methods which are very much in need of improvement. No one can be blamed for this, so long as he remains open to suggestions for improevments and tries to find them himself.

TRADITION AND OBEDIENCE

A number of experiments have been conducted recently into the problem of obedience, the best known being the Milgram tests, originally carried out in America and later repeated in Germany. A psychologist ordered a number of perfectly law-abiding citizens, on the pretext of making a series of tests, to punish people who were unknown to them with electric shocks of increasing intensity, the more mistakes those people made in a series of tasks they had to carry out. Despite the fact that the attention of the subjects was drawn to the danger to health and to the possible consequence of death ensuing from these electric shocks, sixty-two per cent of the tested people followed the instructions of the psychologist conducting the test, even to the point of killing the unknown people, who were, in the test, replaced by dummies. This corresponds very closely to the situation of Abraham who was ready to sacrifice his son Isaac at God's command (Gen. 22). Many modern exegetes interpret this story as a kind of lesson given by God against the then current practice of human sacrifice, but in so doing they fail to answer the question as to how Abraham was able to believe that the order to kill came from God.

This seems to be an example of a process of human evolution which is still in progress and which also has certain parallels in the development of the child. It is not possible to make a child understand at once what is forbidden and what he ought to do, nor is it possible to leave it entirely to him to collect all the necessary experience himself. The child has to learn by means of directions given by adults what he may and may not do. It is only later that he learns to apply himself rationally and critically to the task of assessing these commands and prohibitions. To begin with, we learn emotionally what we have to do. Afterwards, our intellect plays a part and helps us to look for a rational justification.

This may lead us eventually to expect a rational foundation to be found for all traditional knowledge and skills, if enough care is taken to look for it. If this rational basis is not found, then the reason we give is that we lack the necessary insight. Since tradition is present long before intellectual questioning takes place and the human intellect awakes after a long period of growth to find the traditional knowledge already there (both in the evolution of the tribal community and in that of the individual), it is easier to offer pseudorationalizations of tradition than to change it. It may even happen that the rule of behavior may remain unchanged while the justification for it changes. An example of this is the use of the incense, which was laid down in Catholic worship and justified as symbolizing the rising up of prayer to God. In ancient Egypt and Israel, however, where incense was used most lavishly in public worship, the reason was more practical. Burning incense produces phenol or carbolic acid, an antiseptic used as late as the second half of the nineteenth century in operating theaters and elsewhere. In places of worship attended by a great number of people, it was therefore a very suitable means of preventing the spread of infectious diseases. As long as no one sees through the effect mechanism for using incense, then, the experience can certainly be collected, but anyone looking for a rational justification will only answer the question "why?" with "because that is how it has always been." This answer can, of course, be given a higher value by appealing to a higher authority, in which case it will be "because it is God's will."

This trick of appealing to a higher authority always appears whenever those who are convinced of the correctness of what they are teaching cannot produce convincing arguments to justify it, either because they simply do not have them at their disposal or because they do not believe the listener to be able to grasp these arguments. If the reasons used to justify what has to be handed down by tradition become themselves part of the tradition, the recipients of that tradition are bound in the long run to feel undervalued, if their understanding is sufficiently developed, but what is taught does not take this into account. If they lose confidence, then, the teaching authority may try to raise to an even higher level the higher authority appealed to, or to give it a more menacing form. Of course it would be far better to reconsider the entire argument used to justify tradition, even though this might lead less developed people to think that the reasons given in the past were valueless and that they had been deceived. Throughout history, we have seen countless examples of the problems of communication encountered by those putting forward ideas and teachings of every kind, and the same situation prevails today. After all, the degree of previous knowledge possessed by those who have to be taught is different in each case, so that different reasons must be given to each person to justify the same tradition and the same demand.

We might fall back on the fact that everything that is not able to adapt will eventually be eliminated by the process of natural selection, even tradition. Two aspects of this question have, however, to be borne in mind. The first is that this selection of traditions is too slow for us today, because it is no longer so that progress materializes as a single step taken over several generations, but rather that several steps are taken within one and the same generation. If it is true that evolution proceeds much more quickly at this point, then each individual has to examine these ideas and teachings critically for himself, instead of according a higher authority to those views and teachings simply because they are old and traditional, giving new insights a position inferior to that of the earlier views and regarding every change made in the earlier views as inconsistent and questionable.

In the second place, it is important to remember that selection can only operate with what can be tested by its adaptability. What is not biologically and technically adaptive is not subject to natural selection. When evolution proceeds very rapidly, grandparents communicate primarily fairy stories and myths to their grandchildren and not special knowledge or skills. As a consequence, the younger generation comes to think that *all* the tradition that is received from older people consists of fairy stories.

Tradition as the passing on of experiences began, as we have seen, as a process of example and imitation. Children still learn a great deal from their parents precisely in this way: what to eat and how to eat it, whom to call father, aunt, and so on. They accept this information unquestioningly and follow it just as readily. This practice of giving examples is based on a handing on of experience by means of the concrete object and on immediate success. It is therefore less in need of rational justification than traditions which are handed on more abstractly by means of symbols. Thus everything that a child learns directly from its parents by imitation can be accepted without any need for it to be justified in the abstract. Quite the reverse is true, however, in the case of sexual experience, which parents do not include among the examples that they give to their children; it is heavily laden with abstract justifications (which may be meaningful or meaningless). Examples are not given when information or skills are handed on by means of the spoken or written word. This type of tradition has therefore to be justified.

The passing on of experience enables us to learn from the

mistakes made by others. Only a man who could live his life a second time could alone become wise by adversity and at the same time remain capable of competing with others. To rely on the experience of others is called obedience. By relying on others, the individual can be set free, so that the original purpose of obedience is to set the individual free to live a fully human life. Trust is the prerequisite of this obedience, this reliance on others. Blind obedience presupposes complete trust, but, because we know from experience that some authorities are false, mistrust is an attitude which is also necessary. A balanced mixture of trust and mistrust results in a compromise: critical obedience, which we might also call critical disobedience. Blind disobedience and complete mistrust are as unbiological as blind obedience and complete trust. It is impossible to say whether the ideal of trusting everyone because everyone follows the commandment to love his neighbor can be reconciled with the data of human biology, but it is certainly not contrary to human biology to try to achieve this ideal.

Love Your Neighbor as Yourself

THE natural scientist and above all the ethologist is not surprised, but only pleased to learn that the commandments which aim to guide human behavior have a biological basis. Again and again in this book we have encountered one demand which is characteristically human and which is made whenever a living organism endowed with consciousness and spirit emerges at the biological level. This is the frequently quoted commandment found in the code of law which began at the time of Moses and was completed by 450 B.C., the book of Leviticus: "You shall love your neighbor as yourself" (Lev. 19. 18).

Man should not use his fellow man as a tool, as a means to an end, and he should not manipulate him unless he has obtained his consent to do so.[51] Doctors constantly find themselves in the fringe and exception areas of this commandment because of certain therapeutic treatments that are used. The same applies to parents and teachers in their educational methods. These aspects of the problem cannot be discussed here, but they are always due to the fact that those who are treated in this way are insufficiently informed and are often incapable of being informed more completely. The permitted limits of treatment, influence or manipulation of others are not crossed by technical possibilities, but simply and solely by the intention behind their use.

I have already drawn attention to the fact that the permitted limits in sexual behavior are greatly influenced and even shifted by the degree to which the husband treats his

186

wife as a fully human and equal partner. (It is precisely the same with regard to the wife's treatment of her husband, although this is less of a problem in Western society.) The limits to which the exercise of authority can be allowed to go also vary according to the degree of biological maturity reached by the human person, between the first stage of infancy, when he is still incapable of partnership, and the final stage of physical adulthood. But since adults too have to be educated to social partnership, the educational methods and the penalties which may have to be applied have to be geared less towards the age than towards the degree of social maturity achieved by the person being educated. Above all, education and punishment have to be related to the future and to the personal development of the other. It is undeniably immoral to punish, for example, simply and solely for the purpose of resocialization, for this type of punishment only aims to permit society to function with as little friction as possible, even though this may leave the rights of the individual completely out of account. It is equally immoral to punish criminals simply and solely as a deterrent to others, because this reduces the person punished to the stature of an object. I believe that the word "partnership" is really no more than a modern translation of the ancient, but in no sense outdated concept, "love of one's neighbor."

Individual human beings are also, from the purely biological point of view, divided into different groups. As soon as a living organism is capable of knowing, recognizing and distinguishing individuals, this ability can be placed at the service of group living. It also leads inevitably to the existence of two different categories belonging to the same species. These are the members of one's own species who belong to one's own group and the aliens who belong to the same species, but to other groups. It would seem as though this division into different, specialized groups leads to an elimination of competition. Even single homogeneous groups of human beings tend almost always to divide themselves into at least two subgroups which differ in their interpretation of shared traditions.[47]

Two different and in many respects quite opposing moral principles have emerged as a result of this division into groups, one principle governing behavior towards one's own social group, the other determining the attitude within this closed group towards those outside it. The commandment to love one's neighbor becomes problematical as soon as it is extended to those outside the closed group and to those hostile to it. Two different sets of components of the human conscience play a part in this. The emotional component acts as the guardian of correct behavior toward one's own biological group and its voice is heard at once by every member of the group. The voice of the other part of the conscience, on the other hand, the intellectual component, is generally not heard until it is deliberately questioned.

The Italian journalist, Oriana Fallaci, took part in an American dive-bombing raid in Vietnam. She described her reactions in a report. "The third time I had come to terms with the experience and was determined not to miss the moment when Andy released the bombs. I didn't miss it this time and followed everything exactly as it happened . . . By the fourth time I was used to it and the fifth and sixth times I could easily follow it with a certain detachment. It was like a play in which the actors were little figures who ran out of bunkers and sand-bagged barricades beating their arms to free themselves from the flames. One of them was suffocating in the flames. I would be lying if I were to say that I felt any guilt or sympathy. I was completely possessed by the desire that Andy should do what he had to do—to kill so as not to be killed. I had no time

188

to be sorry for them. And I didn't want to either. We were a thousand feet up and I knew we were safe when I saw Martell dive down. I felt a prick, far less than a pinprick. It was so light that it is hardly worth mentioning. That pinprick was not my conscience, but an intellectual desire to be stirred by my conscience."

It is more than unfortunate that we should ever regard this intellectual component as "hardly worth mentioning." It is regrettable that we should only notice the emotional part of our conscience, which is directed towards maintaining the respectability of the group to which we belong and which is regarded by theologians as innate. This part of the conscience is present in social vertebrates[52] at least in the negative form of a "bad" conscience, but it is not sufficient to enable us to observe the Ten Commandments.

The remarkable appendix to this commandment—"you shall love your neighbor *as yourself*"—is not simply an embellishment exempting anyone who cannot bear himself from the obligation to love others. On the contrary, it points to a particularly human characteristic and shows us the biologically prescribed path along which man can fulfil the commandment to love his fellow man.

Man is not only distinguished from all other living organisms in that he learns by tradition handed on by means of symbols, speech and writing. He is also the only creature with the ability to put himself in the place of another creature, to imagine himself in the situation of a fellow being. What is suggested to us is that we approach the love of our fellow men via self-love. This does not imply that we should first think of ourself and then, if we have the time and the inclination, also think of others. What is meant is that we should constantly endeavor to think ourselves into the role played by everyone else as if we had to take over that role and play it ourself.

Helpful Commandments

IT is generally accepted that nothing should be forbidden that does not have to be forbidden. Yet, as everyone knows, eight of the Ten Commandments are prohibitions, which is in itself of little positive help in any attempt to practice love of one's neighbor. This was clearly revealed in an inquiry carried out by the Institute of Applied Social Sciences in Germany in 1970. The aim of the inquiry was to find out which of twelve modes of behavior listed were regarded as particularly deserving punishment. Subject to the obvious assumption that behavior which makes man's life in society particularly difficult in one way or another deserves above all to be punished, the result of the inquiry was bound to reflect the average current assessment of offenses against love of one's neighbor, the view, in other words, that is representative of "public opinion." Those conducting the inquiry named the actions or modes of behavior which were regarded as punishable, so that we cannot refer to the choice of actions, but only to their relative assessment. The list of actions are arranged below according to the degree to which public opinion held them to be punishable.

1. Cruelty to animals (77%)
2. Driving without a driving license (72%)
3. Drug-taking (72%)
4. Beating one's wife (61%)
5. Beating one's children (60%)
6. Nocturnal breach of the peace (42%)

7. Free love and group sex (26%)
8. Prostitution (25%)
9. Parking offenses (20%)
10. Demonstrations (17%)
11. Conscientious objection to military service (13%)
12. Wearing long hair or a beard (6%)

Cruelty to animals was regarded by a majority of those who took part in the inquiry as more deserving of punishment than, for example, beating a member of one's own family, even though animals do not belong to human society. This is a clear indication that most of those questioned relied on the emotional part of the conscience and put themselves more readily in the place of an animal than in that of a fellow human being, who may, of course, even be a competitor. It is also fairly clear evidence of the fact that the propaganda put out by the various societies for the protection of animals based on the principle of respect for life is not intellectual in its appeal. I am not saying anything against the protection of animals as such. I am, however, convinced, on the basis of evidence, that it is not much use as a means to the end of love of one's neighbor.

As a guideline for man's social life today, the results of an inquiry of the type illustrated above are also of limited use. It would not be wrong to say that man prefers commandments to prohibitions and constructive comments to rebukes. Professor H. Klomps of the University of Cologne recently compiled a list of the twenty qualities which were most worth striving to achieve because they represented moral and social fitness. He called these qualities "modern virtues." I would like to end this book by quoting Professor Klomps' twenty modern qualities as a positive interpretation of the Ten Commandments.[27]

1. Sense of responsibility, coupled with a willingness to accept responsibility

191

2. Tolerance (love of truth and maintenance of love of one's neighbor)

3. Love of peace and readiness to compromise and, if necessary, to renounce

4. Objectivity (correct association with things, facts and situations as the modern form of piety)

5. Openness (the attempt to remain spiritually and mentally young)

6. Impartiality (the absence of prejudice)

7. Respect

8. Courage (to stand up for one's own convictions or for those who are weaker and are being treated unjustly, without being intimidated by those who are stronger)

9. Collegiality (willingness to cooperate with others and to put one's own personal ambitions in second place and to accept professional tasks that have to be carried out with others as equally important)

10. Sociability (the cultivation of one's free time in recreation instead of seeking diversion and entertainment, playing about or simply sulking and grumbling)

11. Discretion (caution in speech and restraint with regard to the private lives of others)

12. Restitution (cooperation in the elimination of the consequences of guilt)

13. Shared joy as the necessary complement of shared suffering or sympathy

14. Friendliness (the ability to be spoken to easily by others)

15. Serenity (an inner freedom in one's attitude towards the consequences of reality)

16. Thankfulness (as a free personal response to helping and giving without any obligation; this also includes freely asking)

17. Reliability (objectivized faithfulness)

18. Self-control
19. Patience (inner courage)
20. Humility (readiness to serve others).

Professor Klomps includes no positive or direct references to many of the familiar elements contained in the earlier lists of sins; no mention, for example, is made of sexuality. This is clearly because what he is above all concerned with here are the higher values. All the feelings that fill man's often one-sided overscrupulous conscience are subordinate to these values. I sincerely believe that it might be more helpful for us to learn these twenty modern virtues and to call them to mind from time to time than simply to repeat the traditional Ten Commandments by heart.

Bibliography

1. Arendt, H.: *Macht und Gewalt*. R. Piper & Co., Munich, 1970.
2. Beitl, R.: *Der Kinderbaum*, G. Grote'sche Verlagsbuchhandlung, Berlin, 1942.
3. Biocca, E.: *Yanoáma*, E. P. Dutton & Co., New York, 1970.
4. Bjerre, J.: *Kalahari*, Brockhaus, Wiesbaden, 1960.
5. Boratov, P. N.: *Türkische Volksmärchen*, Akademie-Verlag, Berlin, 1967.
6. Brown, L.: *Eagles*, A. Barker Ltd., London, and Arco Publishing Co. Inc., New York, 1970.
7. Coccola, R. de, and P. King: *Ayorama*, Oxford U. Press, New York, 1956.
8. Coulson, J. C.: "The Influence of the Pair-Bond and Age on the Breeding Biology of the Kittiwake Gull, *Rissa tridactyla*," *Journal of Animal Ecology*, 35 (1966), pp. 269–279.
9. Daettwyler, O., and M. Maximoff: *Tsiganes*, Büchergilde Gutenberg, Zurich, 1959.
10. Eibl-Eibesfeldt, I.: *Grundriss der vergleichenden Verhaltensforschung*, R. Piper & Co., Munich, 1969.
11. ————: *Love and Hate*, Holt, Rinehart & Winston, New York, 1972.
12. Elkin, A. P.: *The Australian Aborigines*, Natural History Press, New York, 1964.
13. Espinas, A.: *Des sociétés animales*, Baillière, Paris, 1878.
14. Estes, R. D.: "Territorial Behavior of the Wildebeest," *Zeitschrift für Tierpsychologie*, 26 (1969), pp. 284–370.
15. Frank, F.: *APO und Establishment aus biologischer Sicht*, G. Stalling, Oldenburg and Hamburg, 1969.
16. Freuchen, P.: *Book of the Eskimos*, The World Publishing Company, Cleveland and New York, 1961.
17. Gabus, J.: *Völker der Wüste*, Walter Volten and Freiburg, 1957.

18. Gwinner, E.: "Über einige Bewegungsspiele des Kolraben," *Zeitschrift für Tierpsychologie*, 23 (1966), pp. 28–36.
19. Haag, H.: "Der Dekalog," in *Moraltheologie und Bibel*, ed. J. Stelzenberger, F. Schöningh, Paderborn, 1964, pp. 9–38.
20. Heiligenberg, W.: "Ein Versuch zur ganzheitsbezogenen Analyse des Instinktverhaltens eines Fisches," *Zeitschrift für Tierpsychologie*, 21 (1959), pp. 1–52.
21. Hermanns, M.: *Die Familie der A Mdo-Tibeter*, Karl Alber, Freiburg and Munich, 1959.
22. Hildebrand, D. von: *The Trojan Horse in the City of God*. Franciscan Herald, Chicago, 1970.
23. Illies, J., in C. Meves and J. Illies: *Lieben—was ist das?*, Herder, Freiburg, Basel and Vienna, 1970.
24. Immelmann, K.: "Vergleichende Beobachtungen über das Verhalten domestizierter Zebrafinken in Europa und ihrer wilden Stammform in Australien," *Zeitschrift für Tierpsychologie*, 77 (1962), pp. 198–216.
25. Jay, P.: "Aspects of Maternal Behavior among Langurs," *Annals of the New York Academy of Science*, 102 (1962), pp. 468–476.
26. Kainz, F.: *Die "Sprache" der Tiere. Tatsachen—Problemschau —Theorie*, Ferdinand Enke, Stuttgart, 1961.
27. Klomps, H.: *Tugenden des modernen Menschen*, Winfried-Werk, Augsburg, 1969.
28. Kropotkin, P.: *Mutual Aid, a Factor in Evolution*, Wm. Heinemann, London, 1902.
29. Kummer, H.: *Social Organisation of Hamadryas Baboons*, S. Karger, Basel and New York, 1968.
30. —————, and F. Kurt: "A Comparison of Social Behavior in Captive and Wild Hamadryas Baboons," in *The Baboon in Medical Research*, ed. H. Vagtborg, University of Texas Press, 1965.
31. Lawick-Goodall, J. van: "The Behavior of Free-living Chimpanzees in the Gombe Stream Reserve," *Animal Behavior Monographs*, 1 (1968), pp. 161–311.
32. Leyhausen, P.: "Zur Naturgeschichte der Angst," in K. Lorenz and P. Leyhausen, *Antriebe tierischen und menschlichen Verhaltens*, R. Piper & Co., Munich, 1968.
33. Lilienfeld, P. von: *Gedanken über die Sozialwissenschaft der*

Zukunft, Part I: *Die menschliche Gesellschaft als realer Organismus,* Georg Reimer, Berlin, 1901.

34. Lorenz, K.: "Der Kumpan in der Umwelt des Vogels," *J. Ornithol.,* 83 (1935), pp. 137–413.

35. ————: "Moral-analoges Verhalten geselliger Tiere," *Forschung und Wirtschaft,* 4 (1954), pp. 1–23; reprinted with the same title in *Universitas,* 11/17 (1956), pp. 691–704.

36. ————: *On Aggression,* Harcourt, Brace & World, 1966.

37. ————: *Evolution and Modification of Behavior,* University of Chicago Press, Chicago, 1965.

38. Marshall Thomas, E.: *Meine Freunde die Buschmänner,* Ullstein, Berlin, 1962.

39. Matthiessen, P.: *Das verborgene Tal,* Droemer Knaur, Munich, 1962.

40. McDougall, W.: *Psychology. The Study of Behavior,* Oxford University Press, New York, 1959.

41. Meisser, U. M.: "Tiersprichwörter und Verhaltensforschung," *Studium Generale,* 22 (1969), pp. 861–889.

42. Merker, M.: *Die Masai,* Johnson Reprint Company, New York and London, 1968.

43. Milgram, S.: "Einige Bedingungen von Autoritätsgehorsam und seiner Verweigerung," *Zeitschrift für experimentelle und angewandte Psychologie,* 13 (1966), pp. 433–463.

44. Mitscherlich, A.: *Bis hierher und nicht weiter. Ist die menschliche Aggression unbefriedbar?,* R. Piper & Co., Munich, 1968.

45. Miyadi, D.: "Differences in Social Behavior among Japanese Macaque Troops," in *Neue Ergebnisse der Primatologie,* ed. D. Starck, R. Schneider, H.-J. Kuhn; G. Fischer, Stuttgart, 1967, pp. 228–231.

46. Mohl, M.: *Einmal Afrika und zurück bitte,* Bertelsmann, Gütersloh, 1965.

47. Möller, H.: "Gemeinschaft, Folk Society und das Problem der 'kleinen Gemeinde,'" *Acta Ethnol. Europ.* 135–145 [1964/-1965).

48. Oosterwal, G.: *Die Papua. Von der Kultur eines Naturvolks,* Kohlhammer, Stuttgart, 1963.

49. Petrucci, R.: "Les origines naturelles de la propriété," *Notes*

et mémoires, Institut Solvay, Travaux de l'Institut Sociologique, Fasc. 3 (Misch et Thon, Brussels, 1905).

50. ————: "Origine polyphylétique." Homotypie et non-comparabilité directe des sociétés animales," *ibid.,* Fasc. *I.*

51. Rahner, K.: *Freiheit und Manipulation in Gesellschaft und Kirche,* Münchener Akademie-Schriften, Vol. 53, Kösel, Munich, 1970.

52. Rauh, F.: *Das sittliche Leben des Menschen im Lichte der vergleichende Verhaltensforschung,* Butzon & Bercker, Kevelaer, 1969.

53. Rensch, B.: *Homo sapiens. Vom Tier zum Halbgott,* Vandenhoeck & Ruprecht, Göttingen, 1970.

54. Rowell, T. E., R. A. Hinde and Y. Spencer-Booth: " 'Aunt'-Infant Interaction in Captive Rhesus Monkeys," *Animal Behavior,* 12 (1964), pp. 219–226.

55. Rüppell, G.: "Eine 'Lüge' als gerichtete Mitteilung beim Eisfuchs (Alopex lagopus L.)," *Zeitschrift für Tierpsychologie,* 26 (1969), pp. 371–374.

56. Schüller, B.: "Wieweit kann die Moraltheologie das Naturrecht entbehren?" *Lebendiges Zeugnis,* 1/2 (1965), pp. 41–65.

57. Seger, I.: *Knaurs Buch der modernen Soziologie,* Droemer Knaur, Munich, 1970.

58. Silberbauer, G. B.: *Bushman Survey Report,* Bechuanaland Press [PTY] Ltd., Mafeking, South Africa, 1965.

59. Southwick, C. H.: *Primate Social Behavior,* Van Nostrand Co., Inc., New York, 1963; see the articles by Imanishi, Kawamura and Itani.

60. Storr, A.: *Lob der Aggression,* Econ Verlag, Düsseldorf, 1970.

61. Süssmilch, J. P.: *Die göttliche Ordnung in den Veränderungen des menschlichen Geschlechts, aus der Geburt, Tod und Fortpflanzung desselben,* J. C. Spener, Berlin, 1741.

62. Thielcke, G., and H.: "Beobachtungen an Amseln (Turdus merula) und Singdrosseln (T. philomelos)," *Die Vogelwelt,* 85 (1964), pp. 46–53.

63. Thorpe, W. H.: *Learning and Instinct in Animals,* Methuen & Co. Ltd., London, 1963.

64. Tinbergen, N.: "On War and Peace in Animals and Man," *Science,* 160 (1968), pp. 1411–1418.

65. Urbain, A.: "Leçon inaugurale du cours d'éthologie des

animaux sauvages," *Arch. Mus. hist. nat.*, series 6, 12, 295–308 (1935).
66. Waxweiler, E.: "Esquisse d'une sociologie," *Notes et Mémoires, Institut Solvay, Travaux de l'Institut Solvay Sociologique*, Fasc. 2, Misch et Thon, Brussels, 1906.
67. Wendler, G.: "Ein Analogmodell der Beinbewegungen eines laufenden Insekts," *Kybernetik*, 1968, Beiheft zu "Elektronische Rechenanlagen" 18 (1968), pp. 68–74.
68. Wickler, W.: *Stammesgeschichte und Ritualisierung. Zur Entstehung tierischer und menschlicher Verhaltensmuster*, R. Piper & Co., Munich, 1965.
69. ————: "Vergleichende Verhaltensforschung und Phylogenetik," in *Die Evolution der Organismen*, Vol. 1, ed. G. Heberer, G. Fischer, Stuttgart, 1967, pp. 420–508.
70. ————: "Socio-sexual Signals and their Intraspectific Imitation among Primates," in *Primate Ethology*, ed. D. Morris, Weidenfeld and Nicholson, London, 1967.
71. ————: *Sind wir Sünder? Naturgesetze der Ehe*, Droemer Knaur, Munich, 1969.
72. ————: *Breeding Aquarium Fish*, Van Nostrand-Reinhold, New York, 1966.
73. ————: "Soziales Verhalten als ökologische Anpassung," *Verhandlungen der zoologischen Gesellschaft*, Cologne (1970), pp. 291–304.

BETHANY
COLLEGE
LIBRARY

DISCARD